A Big Journey

By Rebecca R. Ryan

To Steve & Shawn,
I love you both
so much. Thank you
for your support.
♡ Bex

In Deep Gratitude

I would like to thank Jesus Christ, my Lord and Savior for loving me even when I was underserving of love; for choosing me to be his servant, and giving me Grace beyond measure. Without his presence in my life I would not have become a new creation.

Thank you, Sue Palmer, my editor. Your friendship, encouragement, and dedication to God's vision for this book is truly appreciated. I look forward to working with you for years to come.

I would like to thank my *Jesus Did it* ministry team. Our daily conversations and prayers have been encouraging. Israel Wendy - Thank you for the girl talk and always praying for me. Jason Wallace - Thank you for being my brother and growing with me (you and Pam Wallace are a great hope for me). Joshua Ello - Thank you for always holding me accountable and having real conversations with me. Rick Costa - Thank you for always having my back and encouraging me in times of trial. Thank you for seeing all the ugly sides of me and loving me anyway. You can find more about the Jesus Did It team at www.jesusdidit.org

I would love to thank The Young Family for making me their Auntie. Although we are not blood, you are my family and I love each of you deeply. Josh - Thank you for being my favorite; stay sweet. Jessie -

Thank you for being my mini me; stay beautiful.
Alyssa - Thank you for being unapologetically you;
stay a dreamer. Peter - Thank you for always
speaking truth, stay honorable. Scott - Thank you for
always having corny jokes with me that drive
ChristeneEss crazy and being my brother; stay
snarky. To my best friend, ChristineEss Young -
Thank you for loving me right where I was and for
being a true friend/sister. Thank you for welcoming
me into your family and being patient with me. You
mean more to me than I can express in words

To my sister, Susan Lechuga -- Thank you for
living through the traumatic life events with me. I love
you very much. We will always have a special bond.

My grateful thanks also go to:

- Linda Grossruck- Thank you for accepting me
  in your family and loving me unconditionally.
- Charlie Ryan - Thank you for giving me hope
  throughout my life. You were the light in dark
  days. You are not just an uncle to me you are
  my BUB.
- Sue Spangler - Your love and support mean
  the world to me. The times I spent with you
  growing up showed me what love looks like.
  Thank you for being my aunt and friend.
- Zalmenta Lyon - Thank you for always holding
  me in prayer. I appreciate our deep
  conversations and our sisterly bond.

4

- Darcy Defrees - Our connection shows me how much the Holy Spirit works. Thank you for being my friend and my spiritual sister. Your accountability and encouragement in this process has shown me how much God loves us.
- Sarah Roush - Thank you for showing me that I can be loved. Thank you for stepping out and helping a girl you hardly knew. Thank you for giving me my first makeover and showing me what I was worth.
- Thanks also to numerous others, too many to mention, who I hold in my heart. You, too, have my gratitude

To my Weight Watchers® Sunday Morning Group in Tacoma - thank you for sharing your journeys with me, as well as for the hugs, laughs, and memories. Each one of you are special and encouraging.

Finallly, thank you to everyone who reads this book. I hope it encourages you and helps you realize how much God loves you.

-- *Beckie*

Table of Contents

EMBRACING YOUR NEW IDENTITY

HONESTY: THE BEST POLICY

BEGINNING YOUR HEALTHY RELATIONSHIP WITH FOOD

YOU'VE GOT TO MOVE IT, MOVE IT!

EXECUTING YOUR PLAN

WHERE IT ALL BEGAN

"God is within her, she will not fail...."

Psalm 46:5

I have always been extremely obese.

In fact, at one point, I was told by a psychologist that I identified with the persona of a "big girl." For a long time, their assessment was definitely true.

My obesity impacted every area of my life: relationships, work, finances, and emotions. I longed to find a way out. For years, I studied every fad diet plan that came out and sought to implement them. Try as hard as I might, however, I could not stay with any system longer than a week or two.

Often I would cry to my father about my weight. His response was always the same. "All of us in our family are fat, Beckie. That's just who you are." No matter how much I worked to accept myself that way, however, the world still rejected me.

I was often bullied at school because I looked different from the other girls. Then, when I was in the fifth grade, I overheard some normally sized girls talking about sucking in their stomachs to make themselves look thinner. "If these smaller, prettier girls think they're fat," I told myself, "there's something seriously wrong with me." This, sadly, was the start of a 25-year battle with my unhealthy relationship to food. For years I struggled with binge eating, anorexia, fad diets, and mental abuse. No matter what I did, however, I could not shed the weight.

My mother, who was obese, as well, projected her insecurities on the rest of her family. She often called me fat and lazy, and sometimes even became physically abusive. I could tell she did not love herself. Therefore, I would later realize, she could not love me, either.

We had a lot of financial stress while I was growing up, as well. At times we even went without food. This environment created an unhealthy relationship with food for me. When I became an adult and could afford food, I made sure I ate. Unfortunately with no nutritional knowledge, I often chose fast food or experimented with the latest fad diets. I desperately wanted not to be fat but I became comfortable in the misery and continued to feed the depression – literally -- with pizza.

After a while, faced with repeated failures to end obesity's hold on me, I began simply accepting the persona of "The Big Girl" as an unchangeable reality in my life. I worked hard to accept a "Big is Beautiful" perception of myself. At my core, however, I was still in pain. Being teased at school, growing up in a hoarder home, living with a father who was a closeted homosexual, and experiencing my parents' divorce laid my life's foundation in suffering. My pain continued in adulthood, as I became a victim of domestic violence, was cheated on, experienced bankruptcy, had a miscarriage, was divorced twice, robbed and raped, lost my mom in a car accident and my dad from cancer, all before the age of 33.

When even my second husband, one who had loved my larger size, left me, on October 15, 2015, I was devastated! That same day my boss pulled me into her office, where she reprimanded me for overusing humor in the workplace. I broke down right in front of her, then went home and cried in my closet. I desperately wanted the pain to be gone. Once again, thoughts of suicide consumed me.

Up to this point, I had been agnostic and practiced Jainism, a nontheistic religion which taught that salvation was achieved by becoming perfect through successive lives. That belief, however, had done nothing to relieve my pain. It certainly was doing nothing for me now. So I cried out to God, asking Him, if He was real, to show Himself to me.

God heard my cry and, that very day, told me that Jesus was the way, At first, I laughed. Then I clearly heard God say, "You have done it your way for 33 years. Let Me take over." That night I truly gave my life to Jesus and my transformation began.

The weight I carried that day to the foot of the Cross, both mental and physical, was so deep that I actually needed a powerful deliverance to ultimately set me free. Deliverance is a process filled with a lot of self-examination, prayer, tears, but mostly grace from God and yourself.

In this book I will share with you my testimony of healing, deliverance and freedom, giving you details of how God helped set me free, not only from the obesity that had plagued me all my life but from the underlying emotional issues that kept me bound for years. I will show you the steps God walked me through to heal.

Make no mistake! This will be a *BIG* journey, sometimes even a difficult one, but remember: you are not graded on the outcome. You will not fail, no matter how long or hard your situation has been. That's because God will be with you!

Through this 30-step process, you will establish a plan for success. Each day there will be an exercise for you to complete that will help you find release and redemption, as you walk with Jesus to ultimate freedom physically, emotionally and spiritually. Come on! Let's get started!

" And Moses said to the people, "Do not be afraid. Stand still, and see the salvation of the Lord, which He will accomplish for you today. For the Egyptians whom you see today, you shall see again no more forever. The Lord will fight for you, and you shall hold your peace."

Exodus 14:13-14

ESTABLISHING A FIRM FOUNDATION

Step 1: The Importance of Surrender

" Come to Me, all you who labor and are heavy laden, and I will give you rest. Take My yoke upon you and learn from Me, for I am gentle and lowly in heart, and you will find rest for your souls. For My yoke is easy and My burden is light."

Matthew 11:28-30

Some people believe that surrender is an easy thing to do; just give up and let someone else take control. This is, however, the most difficult step a person can tale. It is also the first step in the journey you have just begun. To surrender means not only giving God control but allowing Him to fight for you. You are fighting for the truth of who God has designed you to be.

Being unhealthy is a by-product of a deeper spiritual battle. In my life, that battle was rooted in many painful experiences. I grew up being ridiculed at school, tormented at home, and constantly comparing myself to the women the world says are beautiful. I desired to be loved and comforted my lonely, fearful heart with food. My size was a blanket of safety. I thought if I were big no one could harm me physically or sexually.

When I was a preteen, I noticed the boys did not look at me as they would other girls in school. I wanted my own family and to be loved like the movies portrayed. Most of all, I wanted a way out of the hellish life my parents created.

My parents rarely had food for breakfast or in the house, period. The shelves were filled with Diet Pepsi®, Doritos®, oatmeal cream pies, and butter pecan ice cream. As bad as those choices were, we weren't allowed to consume anything except the Diet Pepsi®. The rest was our mother's food. If she did not have her "treats," she would become hysterical. In fact, the only meal I ever ate growing up was dinner, and that was usually fast food. As a result, my body was programmed to go for long periods of time without food. It's amazing to think I still became obese, but I did.

Following my freshman year of high school, I attended a music camp that was far enough away from home that I had to live there. This meant I had to eat meals in front of others, so I just didn't eat. After the fourth day, my body could not take any more and I collapsed on the field. Luckily my dad was a chaperon at the camp so he was able to talk to me. When I shared my anxiety over eating in front of others, my cry for help was ignored. Instead of getting me the help I needed, my father told me to "act better" so that he and my mom were perceived to be properly caring for us. They did not want anyone to know that we were living in filth, not being fed consistently, enduring beatings on a daily basis from our mother, and suffering through emotional abuse.

Because of the neglect and abuse I suffered, I became depressed and suicidal. My cries for help went on unheeded until, eventually, I just stopped asking. Food was the only thing that brought me comfort. My size became a blanket of safety. I thought if I were big no one could harm me physically or sexually.

At the same time, however, I hungered for love and desired to be thin. I had no idea how to feed my body, though, so I went through years of starving myself for three to four days at a stretch, then binge eating. When these attempts failed to achieve the results I wanted, I started to believe I was going to be fat my entire life. What's more, I thought everyone lived like this.

At the age of 17, while I was still obese and wearing size 22 (US) women's clothing, I met my first husband. I was thrilled that someone loved me and gave me attention, after being bullied my entire life both in school and at home. I finally was able to start eating regularly and tried to take care of myself. He thought I was beautiful.

I felt "seen" as I had never been seen before. It was heaven compared to the life I had been living and, within two years of meeting him, we were married. He was my hero. I would have done anything for him - and I did. My dreams were finally coming true.

Then one day I found a pornographic photo of a skinny woman on his computer. I was devastated, not only because he was involved with such things but because, more important to me, that picture told me I was not the type of woman my husband truly desired.

In a desperate attempt to save my marriage, I started starving myself so I could become the woman he wanted me to be. He had saved me from a terrible home and I felt I owed him perfection. Sadly, my efforts to become perfect only resulted in causing me to gain even more weight. No one knew I had an issue with not eating since I was still obese.

Along with the poor nutrition, starving myself also caused stress in my emotions. Soon I became suicidal. Regularly I would go into fits of major depression.

Meanwhile, my husband had gone from just viewing pornography to actually looking for women on dating sites. This led to an affair and finally abandonment, when he chose to leave me for the other woman he had found. I felt my world collapse around me. I fell into a deep, dark depression and slept with men just to ease the pain I suffered from believing I was undesirable. I did not value my body or myself, yet, deep inside, I was yearning to find love.

I spent the next six months partying, dating recklessly, binge eating, and believing it was all I deserved. Underneath it all, though, I was desperate to prove I was lovable and cherished. Then I met my second husband. He loved big women, so when he proposed, I immediately agreed. We were married nine months after meeting.

Never in my life did I feel more desired or wanted but the entire marriage, I would later realize, was built on lust, not love, for him. When he tired of me, he left me for another woman. Again I felt unlovable and again I turned to food for solace. I shut off the entire world and did the bare minimum: work, eat, sleep.

Desperately in that forgotten place I cried out to God and accepted Jesus as my Lord and Savior. When I did so, I did not know how much that decision would impact my life. I had to learn to let God love me and remove the idea that God was the cause for my pain. I had to surrender all my past hurts and become vulnerable.

Surrendering was difficult for me. I believed if I did not hold on to the pain, those who had abused me would get away with it. in order to heal my hurt, however, and truly experience freedom, I had to let God remove my victim mentality. I needed to stop using what had happened to me to excuse my weight issues. I had to allow God to remove all the sorrow. I had to surrender every belief I had about my life -- my past, the abuse, the pain, the anger -- and surrender my understanding of these things to God.

Step 1 Activity: The Importance of Surrender

Use the space below to list some beliefs you have that you need to surrender to God. (For me, these beliefs included that I was unlovable, that I would always be fat, that everyone was going to hurt me, and that God did not care.) Do not worry about how they look; be honest.

1. _____

2. _____

3. _____

4. _____

5. _____

Now take a moment to pray and ask God to take these burdens. These are not your truth. God's Word is truth. My prayer was simple: "Lord I know I am angry and hurt. Take this burden from me and help me to see myself through your eyes. Remove the lies of the enemy from me and help me to first love you and then love myself. In Jesus' Name, Amen."

Remember to compare your list to what the Bible says about you. Does your list match what the word of God says? If not, renounce it right away and begin working to let go of these false beliefs whenever they come to mind

You may need to repeat this exercise many times throughout your journey. I still go through this process.

→
Perfect for Thanksgiving leftovers

Knife-and-fork Italian turkey & pepper sandwich

Prep 15 min | Cook 8 min
Serves 1

 3

1 tsp extra-virgin olive oil
1 cup sliced sweet red and yellow bell peppers
½ cup sliced onion
2 medium garlic cloves, minced
½ tsp fennel seed
½ tsp dried oregano
½ cup shredded cooked skinless turkey breast
1 small tomato, cut into chunks (¾ cup)
Pinch salt
1 oz Italian bread, toasted
2 Tbsp sliced fresh basil

HEAT oil in medium nonstick skillet over medium-high heat. Cook peppers and onion, stirring occasionally, until golden, about 5 minutes.

STIR in garlic, fennel seed, and oregano; cook, stirring, 30 seconds. Add turkey; toss to coat. Stir in tomato and salt; cook, stirring occasionally, until tomatoes soften and are heated through, 1-2 minutes. Spoon on top of toast and sprinkle with basil.

 Nut-free

PHOTOGRAPHY: DAVID MALOSH (SANDWICH), JEN GRANTHAM (PIE)

WW Weekly

November 25—
December 1, 2018

Reality check the holidays

'Tis the season for rich food, parties, and family time. Even when you have a plan, the holidays often pull you in many directions. How best to respond so you can enjoy this time of year?

WHAT TO DO
Shift your thinking

The way you think affects what you do. Imagine your boss invites you to a party the same night as your son's recital. If you think that skipping the party means you won't get a promotion, you'll probably get stressed out–and you might wind up overextending yourself or eating for comfort. Instead, do a reality check. Press pause and focus on the facts to shift unhelpful thoughts to realistic, helpful ones.

Unhelpful thought: "If I don't go to the party, he'll think I'm not dedicated so I won't get the promotion we've discussed."

Reality check: "Is there evidence that he'll think I'm not dedicated? No. He knows how hard I work."

Helpful thought: "I'm disappointed I can't make the party, but that says nothing about my job dedication."

THIS WEEK
Do a reality check

Using the example above, think of a holiday challenge you might face. Write an unhelpful thought you could have; give it a reality check and write a more helpful thought.

My reality check

Unhelpful thought: ....

Reality check: ....

Helpful thought: ....

For more ways to reality-check unhelpful thoughts, see this week's e-newsletter or go to ww.com/us/weeklytopic.

Wellness that Works.™

Step 2: Establishing Your Goal

"Commit your works to the Lord, and your thoughts will be established."

Proverbs 16:3

At one point in my life, looking at the scale terrified me. To know my weight would force me to acknowledge I had failed. The number screamed I was not good enough and unworthy of love. When I would go for a doctor's appointment, I would refuse to step on the scale, forcing them to guess my weight. If a more persistent nurse were weighing me in, I would look away and ask her not to repeat the number. My self worth was too invested in the number the scale reflected.

When I was 22, my husband and I decided to start a family. I was having trouble conceiving, so we decided to pay for fertility treatments. At the fertility clinic, I learned I had polycystic ovarian syndrome (PCOS). It was this condition and my morbid obesity (I then weighed 338 pounds), the doctor told me, which were preventing me from conceiving.

I felt like a failure, both as a wife and a human being. When my husband learned about my fertility problems, he made matters worse: *"So you're really not even a woman then," he commented cruelly.* The weight of those words burned for many years and jump started my pattern of starving myself, then binge eating.

This time I was weighing myself two times a day, with the number on the scale determining if I were allowed to eat. I became obsessed with the scale to a frightening degree. "If I become and give him a baby," I thought, "He will love me and we will finally be happy. Our issues will be resolved."

I was eventually able to get down to 299 pounds. Unfortunately, about this time, I lost my mother in a freak car accident. It was just too much and I quit caring about myself entirely. My relationship with my mother never had the chance to mend. The physical and mental abuse she had put me through continued to pain me, and now, all hope for healing seemed to have vanished. In an effort to cope, I ate my emotions away. Within a year and a half of my mom's death, my father also died, after a long struggle with cancer.

By the time I was 25, I had lost both my parents. By 28, I had lost all my grandparents, had a miscarriage, and found out my husband was leaving me for another woman because, he told me, I could not give him a baby. My dreams of a family lay in shambles. Life continued to spiral down as I suffered bankruptcy, survived a rape, was forced to file a restraining order against a man I briefly dated, was robbed, and was hospitalized following a suicide attempt.

My weight began to identify me and I gave up. I did not want to live any more. The only comfort I had was food. I could not face the harsh reality that I was killing myself with unhealthy choices. For years, I continued to make bad decisions, all in an effort to find love and acceptance, but they eluded me. No one seemed available to help me through my traumas; pizza was my only comfort. For a brief moment, as I ate, I could forget all my troubles.

I finally gave my life to Jesus on October 15, 2015, and the deliverance process began. For a year and four months, God helped me clear my mind and begin to accept his love. Then, on March 5, 2017, I walked into Weight Watchers to begin my weight loss journey in earnest.

When I first stood on the scale, I dreaded learning the ugly number it would show. Then , I remembered something Maya Angelou had written: *"You can't really know where you are going until you know where you have been."* So I steeled myself to face the truth, even though I thought I would have a nervous breakdown. Amazingly, however, no such reaction occurred. Instead, upon learning that I weighed nearly 400 pounds, I had a sense of peace and determination. I prayed and gave my weight loss journey to God: *"Heavenly Father, I have tried for 35 years to lose weight on my own. Now I give this to You."* Slowly but surely, losing weight would become for me a form of worship to God.

After looking at my height and body type, the weight loss counselor at Weight Watchers and I decided that my goal weight should be 180 pounds, At first I was overwhelmed; I would have to lose over 200 pounds! Unlike other times I'd tried and failed, however, this time I knew God was with me. I had a peace that surpassed understanding and, soon, Matthew 19:26 (NKJV) became my mantra: *" But Jesus looked at them and said to them, "With men this is impossible, but with God all things are possible."*

Step 2 Activity: Establishing Your Goal

Weigh in! If you want to establish a reasonable goal for your journey, it's important to know where you are at the start of your quest. Getting on the scale and facing facts is key. Then establish a goal for your weight loss. Record both below:

On _____ my current weight is _____.
    (Date)

My healthful goal weight is _____.

Next, start a log, tracking your food intake weekly. Establish an exercise program that you can reasonably do each week. I personally use Weight Watchers® to help me keep on track, but there are free alternatives online, as well. Choose whichever plan seems most feasible for you.

Documentation is going to be a huge part of the process. As difficult as taking a picture of your full body is right now, do it anyway. You will thank yourself later. Try to take a picture monthly or at big milestones. I decided to take a picture every 25 pounds or on dates that were significant.

Place your "before" picture here:

This picture does not define me. It is a reminder of where I have been. I promise to take a picture of myself every

_____.
(day of week/month)

**"You *are* all fair, my love,
And *there is* no spot in you."**

Song of Solomon 4:7

Step 3: Finding Out Why

" Or do you not know that your body is the temple of the Holy Spirit who is in you, whom you have from God, and you are not your own? For you were bought at a price; therefore glorify God in your body and in your spirit, which are God's."

1 Corinthians 6:19-20

Before giving my heart to the Lord, being "The Big Girl" was my identity and I strove to embrace that persona. My second husband was a man who loved large women, so when he left, I kept my weight on in an attempt to win him back.

In reality, my weight was used, both before and after my second husband, to attract as well as protect me like a suit of armor. Having gone through tremendous amounts of abuse, I wanted to limit the amount of people who could hurt me.

Strangely, I sometimes even enjoyed being "The Big Girl" because I felt protected by it. Because I was large, I became a social butterfly and was able to make people laugh. I knew every fat joke and would be the first to use them against myself in an effort to prove I was "enough." I figured if they were laughing at a joke, they were not laughing at me. All of this was a smokescreen from the pain I was hiding.

Sadly, every positive thing my large size brought me also caused me more pain. My obesity denied me many opportunities, both at school and after I entered the work force. It also killed my confidence.

While I was in high school, for example, I joined the marching band. This meant, of course, being fitted for a band uniform. I was mortified when the uniform company did not have a women's size that would fit me. Instead, they had to fit me for the largest men's pants size they had.

On another occasion I tried out for a musical. The director told me afterwards that, though my performance had been great, he could not cast me in a lead role due to my size. The chorus line was the only place he could put me; only they had a costume that would fit me.

Throughout the years, such agonizing and hurtful experiences would occur, causing me to recoil deeper and deeper into my shell of fat and fake exuberance. I was continually teased and dismissed for spots in the limelight due to my size.

Nevertheless, even obstacles such as finding clothes to fit me for various occasions, I still went to prom, attended weddings and graduation, and participated in special events. I found stores that would sell my items, wore stretchy clothes and dark colors. I learned to have no embarrassment or shame, even though I knew people were staring at me. Early in my adult life, as I was leaving work, I heard a little boy ask his mom, "Why is that lady so fat?" The first time I heard this, I cried, but after many other occurrences, I just learned to ignore the comments.

I tried to hold my head up high until, one day, I realized my obesity would not only subject me to hurtful comments but it was destroying my career. I was operating as an interim manager for a bank when this realization hit me full force. At the end of my term, confident that my performance as interim manager had been excellence, I applied for the permanent position. To my dismay, I was not selected. The reason shocked me to my core.

"Beckie what do you think of obese people?" my manager asked, as I sat with him in his office. Unsure of what he was trying to say, I said, " I don't know; what do you think?" He was blunt. "Most Americans see obese people as unintelligent, lazy, and not reliable. So, due to your size, we are unable to give you the position." Then he added, "This will hold you back in your career, no matter how good you are on paper."

I left the conference room and cooled down. When I returned, I asked what I could do to overcome this. His answer was simple and direct: "Lose weight."

I spoke with the human resources department. Perhaps they could help. Being overweight certainly couldn't be a real reason for being refused a job. Sadly, I learned that this was not a protected class and I had no rights to pursue a discrimination case, so I quit the job and took a huge pay cut. I had always suspected that my weight was holding me back from promotions and jobs, but, I wasn't certain until my manager spoke those words.

Despite this terrible realization, I still could not find strength enough to change. After a time I started losing my breath just while walking from my car and up eight stairs to my house. I struggled to fit into booths at restaurants, could barely walk to the mailbox, had to use the handicapped stalls in restrooms, and had trouble properly taking care of my hygiene. I could not stand in the shower, clean my house for long periods of time, walk through the grocery store, or cook without having back pain. I was breathing but I wasn't living.

Every time in the past that I had tried to lose weight, I would think about how hard the process was and how I could not move like everyone else. I struggled with feeling defeated and that the battle was too much for me to handle. I would put my best effort in for a few months but, eventually, I would cave in to negative thinking and retreat to the bad habits of eating poorly and being slothful.

The day I finally decided to get the weight off was a normal one. I was experiencing the same struggles as usual but, this time, as I was coming home from work, I asked God to remove all the pain from my heart. Just then, I heard a faint voice say, *"If you love Me so much, why are you killing the body I gave you?"*

His words gave me pause. I'd never thought about my obesity in that way before. Suddenly I realized that the world would not hear how God delivered me from codependency, suicidal thoughts, PTSD, and PCOS seriously while I weighed close to 400 pounds. More importantly, losing weight would enable me to move better, reach more people, travel more, have extra money and most of all, *live longer to serve God.*

Then and there, I handed my weight loss journey over to God. My reason for losing weight had changed dramatically. No longer was it all about me. Instead, it was about becoming a living sacrifice for God. When my reason for losing changed, so did my entire journey. I used my exercise to get closer to God with prayer and ate food which God had designed to nourish me, not merely stuff that merely satisfied a human craving. No longer was my journey a daily battle. Instead, it was an expression of joy and worship of God's love and power.

Step 3 Activity: Finding Out Why

List some things you'd love to do, if only your weight wasn't holding you back. A few of mine included buying my dream car, sitting in a restaurant booth, and fitting comfortably into an airplane seat, without having to use a safety belt extension.

1. _____

2. _____

3. _____

4. _____

5. _____

Now consider what it would mean for you to do these things. What emotions arise in your heart as you think about it. I had always wanted to go sky diving, for example, but when the opportunity to do so arose, I couldn't do it because I weighed over 250 pounds. I felt so rejected.

List five core emotions that place limits on you:

1. _____

2. _____

3. _____

4. _____

5. _____

Now, using the information you've written above, create a mission statement to guide you on your journey. Here's mine: "I want to get healthy so that I am able to serve God and move freely." What is your mission statement?

_____

_____

_____

_____

_____

Step 4: Selecting An Accountability Partner

"Though one may be overpowered by another,
two can withstand him.
And a threefold cord is not quickly broken."

Ecclesiastes 4:12

My first husband and I were best friends; I trusted him completely. We did and shared everything with one another. He was my first love and I believed he would be with me forever. He was my rock as I endured my parents' neglect, abuse and, finally, their deaths. He helped me work through my financial problems. He was my biggest cheerleader when I went to school and, after that, when I started working full time. When he left me for another woman, an essential part of me was crushed beyond recognition. I shut down, and taught myself to never rely on anyone. I didn't think I would ever trust anyone ever again.

Over time, of course, I began dating again and having friendships, but I never let my guard down. Yes I would share some of my story, but I never let anyone see all of me. I did not share my struggles, heartbreaks, or fears. Though I wanted to be free from loneliness, I also feared being victimized again

For years, my laughing, social butterfly persona drew many people around me. Inside, however, I was completely isolated. No one had any idea how someone like me could be so lonely. I was, however, crying for help.

My defenses were so high, in fact, that when I met my first friend at church, I didn't talk to her for six months. I kept her at arm's length because everyone I'd loved before had wounded me in one way or another. When my husband left me, I felt dead inside and vowed to protect myself by keeping part of myself locked away. I would never be so vulnerable and trusting again, I told myself, not even when I decided to remarry.

In December 2015, for my birthday, a friend invited me to her house. I was afraid to fully accept her friendship, but in the months that followed, I slowly came to trust her and we became close. After a while, I felt like I was part of her family. When I shared my life story, she still loved me and walked me through the journey. She accepted me at my absolute lowest. She never tried to change me. She just prayed for me and helped me to see I was worthy of love and acceptance. I shared with her my yearning to lose weight. I never knew how much I needed a friend until I met her. That woman is still my friend today. I know that, no matter what happens, she will keep me grounded.

Shortly after we became friends, I started watching live stream videos on an application called

Periscope©®. One person whose broadcast I watched frequently would sing for the Lord and pray for anyone watching who had need. After a few months of watching, I started broadcasting, as well. Eventually, I teamed up with that other broadcaster, along with a few others, and started an online ministry. This person became another friend that loved me unconditionally without bad intentions.

As I was losing weight, my friend joined me in my efforts and also lost weight. On days where I was discouraged, both my friends would encourage me to keep going. We would compete for the most steps walked in a day and check in with each other on a daily basis.

These two people showed me that I could allow love in. Due to their gift of unconditional acceptance, I found strength to get through times when I thought I could not go on. There were many occasions when I cried on their shoulder. Instead of taking advantage of me in my weakness as others had done before, they encouraged me. Throughout my journey many others encouraged me, as well, but these two people were with me from the beginning. In the dark days they reminded me not to give up on the promise I made to God, myself, or them.

Each accountability partner provided a different type of support. One of my friends met with me weekly to discuss what was happening, not only in our quest for a healthier body and lifestyle but in all of our life goals. We scheduled a time and made the meeting a priority. We also agreed that whenever I was walking in her area I would message her and let her know my location so she could join me if she were available. She also prayed for me continually and I did the same for her. When I would feel depressed or felt like giving up, I would call, and she would remind me of the truth God declared about me and my situation in His Word.

My other friend lived out of state so we would chat daily by phone and check in on each other. We would share how many steps we had walked that day and how our eating habits were going. We encouraged each other to limit our favorite foods. Mine was pizza and theirs was chocolate chip cookies. When I was craving pizza, I would message my friend so that I would not be tempted. There were days I thought I was going to have a bad weigh in. My friend would remind me that the number on the scale did not matter; tomorrow was a new day.

Both of these friends are my accountability partners, vital companions on my journey toward health, wholeness and a fruitful life. While once I tried to walk this journey alone, now I know the important part that faithful friends can play. God has shown me that we are one body. When one body part is hurting, the other parts of the body need to support the broken part.

Eventually as we walked together, I became an inspiration to my friends, as much as they had been to me. I was able to return the encouragement and love they gave me. We truly became partners in this weight loss journey.

At the start of my journey, I battled a lot with fear, rejection and abandonment. I had to learn to be vulnerable with my accountability partners. God showed me that by not allowing people to be there for me, I was taking a blessing away from them.

We shared a lot of tears, my friends and I, but we also experienced a lot of joy. Often the joys outweighed the sorrows. I know we are one body and that Christ wants us to hold up and encourage one another in every aspects of our life. We are not meant to walk through this life alone.

Step 4 Activity: Selecting an Accountability Partner

Choosing the proper accountability partner is important. They should be someone you can be vulnerable with, someone that is committed, above all, to your well-being.

List five traits that you want your accountability partner to have. Some of the traits I sought in my partner was the ability to encourage me, be straight forward, check on me weekly and be a Christian.

1. _____

2. _____

3. _____

4. _____

5. _____

Who are a few people you can ask to be your accountability partner?

_____

_____

_____

Commit to a few people to be your accountability partners. As you go throughout your journey, you will find that you will pick up more partners along the way. List those partners here:

My accountability partners are:

_____

_____

We have agreed to check in every _____.

(Frequency)

THE TRANSFORMATIVE POWER OF LOVE

Step 5: Acknowledging Your Brokenness

"...looking carefully lest anyone fall short of the grace of God; lest any root of bitterness springing up cause trouble, and by this many become defiled...."

Hebrews 12:15

Growing up I would romanticize about my future marriage and husband. I fantasized about the kind of life we would have. We'd live in a three-bedroom house, surrounded by a white picket fence with roses. We'd have two kids (a boy and a girl) and own two cars.

Cinderella was my favorite movie because I felt that I was living the same life. She had lost her parents, was forced to be subservient to people who did not love her, and was, in all meaningful ways, alone. One day she meets a prince. They marry and "live happily ever after."

I would often wonder who my prince would be and prayed that God would send me someone. The line from the movie, *Jerry McGuire©®,* "You complete me," expressed my views on the subject completely. I thought I needed a man to be my prince and complete me.

Being a big girl, I did not get much attention in high school. There was an occasional boyfriend, and dates to the dances did happen, but my entire world shifted when I met my ex-husband. I was 17 years old and desperate for companionship. My own parents had broken up two years earlier, after my dad trying to kill himself, then, revealed he was homosexual. My sister moved to Colorado shortly thereafter and our home life descended into even more chaos. Neither of my parents wanted me but, for financial reasons, I was forced to stay with my abusive mother. Luckily, she worked the night shift so we were like two ships passing in the night.

Emotionally, I had to be there for both my parents during this transition. This meant I acted as the nurturing adult while they behaved like petulant, unhappy children.

My dad was suicidal and I had to save his life a few times before he fully accepted and embraced his homosexual lifestyle. One time I had to perform CPR on him after he strangled himself with an alarm clock cord. Another time I had to talk him out of shooting himself with a loaded gun.

My mother became less violent, but life became more dangerous for me because a lot of the men she brought home would try to force their unwanted attentions upon me. One of her many ex-boyfriends even invited me to live with him, offering to give me a car if I did so.

She went through many men. Then, one year later, she brought home her second husband. We had never even met. Later, because he did not like me, she kicked me out of the house! I couldn't believe it! She had chosen a man she barely knew over her own daughter.

Though now I realize they were working through their hurt and pain, I felt so alone, vulnerable and unloved during those years following my parents' divorce. It was not unusual for me to feel suicidal, particularly during that season. On my 16th birthday I was all alone. My parents forgot and did not do anything special. I pretended it was okay but, inside, I was hurt and humiliated. I just wanted to be loved and cherished like every other girl I knew.

I could not take the burdens of grief and loneliness anymore, so I swallowed half a bottle of aspirin. The label said the pills would bring "pain relief," and that's what I desperately needed right then. I called my dad to say goodbye and he rushed over to make me throw up. My mom also came home from work to help. Since they were fresh out of a divorce, however, they got in a fight and I had to break it up. My dad left and my mom went back to work, leaving me alone again with no help or medical treatment. They were more concerned about themselves than me.

Thankfully, God has since healed me from such suicidal thoughts but, for years, I would suffer with many suicide attempts and feelings. A few times I ended up in the hospital. The root of my self-destructive actions was that I simply did not feel loved or valued by anyone.

I was young, vulnerable and unprotected when I became infatuated with my first husband. We met online and later at a party. He gave me the attention I was lacking and made me feel seen. The day my mom kicked me out of the house, he proposed. Of course, I said yes. I thought he was my rescuing knight in shining armor. Two years later we married. I thought my "happily ever after" had come.

Having been raised in a home filled with abuse, I did not recognize the red flags in our relationship when they were raised. We would barely fight but when we did, he would become abusive and on occasion he would slap me. He even told me he had killed his ex-girlfriend for cheating on him. Still I stayed. Towards the end of our 10-year relationship, I found out he was having an affair. I begged for him to stay with me, but this made him more contemptuous and violent than before. In our final months together, he started beating me on a regular basis.

The final time he hit me was on October 9, 2009. He had just gotten back from a trip with the other woman. I hid his phone and he became angry. When I refused to tell him where his phone was, he nearly strangled me. I was losing my breath, then suddenly he let me go. I am not sure what caused him to stop, but he did. The episode wasn't over, however. He proceeded to beat me, kick me, call me names, and finally, spit on me. He had never called me a name before. That hurt almost worse than his kicks and punches. My "happily ever after" was destroyed. There was nothing I could do could save our relationship, dysfunctional as it was.

I spiraled downward and entered into relationships with many men as I tried to heal my broken heart. I remarried quickly to prove my desirability and value, but I fell into a familiar relationship that again ended in abuse and an affair. Later, God showed me that I had to rely on Him and give Him my broken heart to mend. God would show me how to heal the broken heart and how to allow love in. First, however, I had to acknowledge the betrayal, rejection, abuse, and abandonment.

Step 5 Activity: Acknowledging Your Brokenness

What past pains are you holding on to?

1. _____

2. _____

3. _____

4. _____

5. _____

Describe the first time you felt unloved:

_____

_____

_____

_____

Recognize that this one incident is not an indication of whether you are loveable or not. It will not control your life.

Step 6: Healing Your Brokenness

"For we do not wrestle against flesh and blood, but against principalities, against powers, against the rulers of the darkness of this age, against spiritual hosts of wickedness in the heavenly places."

Ephesians 6:12

On October 15, 2015, in the closet of my bedroom, my life changed forever.

Earlier that morning I had received notification via a postcard from the USPS that my second husband had moved to Georgia without a goodbye. We had been separated for eight months, but I believed we were working on our relationship. Since I had learned from a young age to push through my emotions, I decided to go to work. While there, I received a call from my doctor's office. They had found some abnormalities during my last visit, and they wanted to run some more tests.

When I thought the day could not get worse, I was pulled into the office to speak with my district manager about my over-use of humor at work to cope with my struggles. I lost my composure and started weeping openly in front of her. Consequently she sent me home.

That evening I wanted to die. Literally. I felt as I had when I was a young child. The world was too overwhelming for me. So, like I had done many times in childhood, I climbed into a closet at home and screamed at God: "Why is my life so bad? Why don't You step in? What did I do to deserve this? Where are You?"

After a few hours of debating how I would kill myself and wondering if God even existed (I was practicing Jainism, a nontheistic religion, at the time), I heard His voice speaking to me for the very first time: "You have done it your way for 33 years. Now it is time for you to do it My way." I immediately knew, with shocking clarity, that Jesus was the truth. For years I had not believed it. In fact, I'd spent a great deal of time pointing out the faults in Christianity. I would do that no longer.

The months following this epiphany would be difficult. I spent the holidays and my birthday alone. My broken heart was still ever present but I had a new-found strength and hope inside me that I'd never had before. God started bringing me the support I needed, including an online community of believers and my two friends that would later become my support system.

In order to heal my angry and battered heart, I had to allow God to take all the pain of my life away and trust him, even though I was still angry with Him. I started reading the Bible every day and praying without ceasing. I read every devotional I could get my hands on. I surrounded myself with His love. Whenever the church doors were open, I was there. I even took a class on how to overcome the mental blocks in my life.

I spent the next six months redecorating my house, so I felt a fresh start when I got home. I stopped listening to secular music, overusing sleeping pills, and smoking marijuana to cope with my pain. I decided I did not want to be numb the pain anymore. Instead, I wanted to heal my broken heart. I faced the pain head on. It was brutal. I even attempted suicide a few more times during the process, and had to go to the hospital. Thankfully, God recognized my anguish and carried me through. Healing my broken heart was a process, I realized, with practical steps to help me get through, much like an addict would use to be free.

I came up with a game plan to help me press on whenever I felt overwhelmed. First, I would acknowledge how I was feeling in that exact moment and allow myself to feel everything: the good, bad, and the ugly. I set a time limit on feeling those emotions, and afterwards, I would move along. If I noticed that I was becoming bogged down in a bad mood, I forced myself to reach out to someone and/or get out of my current environment. Because my brokenness often brought on anxiety, I tried different and healthful coping techniques, mechanisms and activities to help calm me down.

One of the most helpful things I did was place reminders of love around my house. I have a statement by my bathroom mirror saying: "I am worthy of love." Every time I go in the bathroom that room, I remind myself I am worthy of love.

Some other techniques I found helpful were:

- The 5,4,3,2,1 Technique: Find five things I can see, four that I can touch, three that I can hear, two that I can smell, and one that I can taste
- Colored in adult coloring books
- Walked
- Went to the movies
- Learned to paint on canvas
- Played my trumpet
- Joined the worship team at church
- Hung out with friends
- Learned to knit
- Took my dog to dog parks

I learned to get out and live life, even though I was in pain. These activities showed me that there was still plenty of joy left in this world, even when I felt as if I could never love again.

I also realized the truth of Ephesians 6:12: "For we do not wrestle against flesh and blood, but against principalities, against powers, against the rulers of [a]the darkness of this age, against spiritual hosts of wickedness in the heavenly places."

My own war was waged mostly against the negative thoughts in my head. When I chose to be happy, I was happy. At first it was a process but, through practice, the moments of tears became less and the times of joy and happiness increased.

Step 6 Activity: Healing Your Brokenness

What are the top five feelings you have trouble shaking?

_____

_____

_____

_____

Write down all the hurt and pains that are impacting you on a piece of paper. Record everything that comes to mind until you cannot think of anything else. Realize there is nothing you can do to change what has happened, but you can change your current mindset about these sufferings. Tear up the paper, then burn it, as a symbolic act of letting go. Now, every time you start to dwell on these issues, remember that you no longer identify with these emotions. They are the past and you choose to leave them there and move forward.

Step 7: Allowing Love In

"And God will wipe away every tear from their eyes; there shall be no more death, nor sorrow, nor crying. There shall be no more pain, for the former things have passed away."

Revelations 21:4

After many failed relationships, I finally realized I was codependent and searching for love. I not only *wanted* the butterflies and romance; I needed them. Men would easily become infatuated with me because of my outgoing personality and how much I lavished attention and affection upon them. In reality, that bubbly persona masked a desperation, cloaked in a pitiful pattern of trying to earn love and acceptance. Many people would *tell* me how much they loved me; what they meant, I would later realize, was that they loved how *I* treated *them*.

I moved across the country twice to make my first husband happy. I felt I *had* to do this. In fact everything I did, from working full time, going to school full time and taking care of all the housework, was done to please my husband. Not surprisingly, I lost much of my own identity in the process.

Regrettably I continued this pattern In my second marriage, sometimes waking up in the middle of the night to prepare dinner for him. (He got home from work at one or two o'clock in the morning.) I drove him to his job so he could sleep later in the mornings. I gave him massages whether I felt like it or not every night. I never wanted to burden either of my spouses with my sorrows, so I kept quiet and pretended to be happy.

Then one September morning in 2008, my husband tried to kill himself by taking an overdose of pain and sleeping pills. My first reaction was to save the man I loved, so, I took over all his worries. I began to smother him with attention. I just wanted him to be happy.

To make matters worse, his suicide attempt happened during a three-year period where I had a devastating miscarriage, lost my mom in a car accident, my dad to cancer, and all my grandparents, as well. My husband and I also lost our house and filed for bankruptcy. Losing our baby was especially difficult for me to bear. I'd waiting a long time to get pregnant. In my grief, I found it impossible to talk to my husband, primarily because I did not want to upset him. Later, I would find out about his affair and suffer through domestic violence.

When my idea of love crumbled, my search for acceptance and love became more desperate. I would get excited by text messages from men I barely knew. At one point I was talking to ten different guys but none of the attention filled the void or eased my loneliness. I was broken and nothing I did to fill my lonely heart seemed to ease my pain. It didn't help that I had built a 10-foot emotional wall that few, if anyone, noticed, let alone could scale. I longed for the satisfaction I knew that deep emotional attachment and affection could bring, but I was afraid to take any risks for fear I would only be hurt again.

It was only as I turned to God, spent time in personal devotions and reading the Bible, that the change I really needed began to happen. I started to realize that I needed to get to know people and take the risk of allowing them to get close to me. God worked on me and helped me, slowly but surely, to become vulnerable with others. It wasn't an easy process. I was like a feral cat, wary and ready to flee, masking my pain when meeting people. God was patient with me, slowly bringing people into my life who could love me as I was. As I took refuge in God, He showered me with love in big ways and small. The breakthrough came as I fixed my eyes on Him and His love for me.

In my front room on a television stand sits a birthday card with a Cinderella theme that says, "Unleash Your Inner Princess." I received it from one of my good friends on my 35th birthday. At the time, this friend and I were only friends online. Still, the card meant the world to me. This was the first birthday card I had received in many years so it arrived completely unexpectedly. Also, my friend didn't know that *Cinderella* was my favorite movie. I asked them why they chose it. "The Holy Spirit told me to choose it," they said. I was deeply moved. This friend had no alternative motive in sending me the card except to show appreciation and love towards me. No one had ever done that for me before.

This would be the first of many such examples of love that people poured over me after I decided to accept gifts of joy and goodness in my life. I had to risk being vulnerable and hurt again to receive it, however. As people showered me with love, my perception of what love was evolved and I learned what true love was. Real love, I learned, involved being vulnerable and trusting people to see you completely. Once I was honest with who I was, I was able to attract people into my life who lifted me up.

Learning to receive true love from also, I soon learned, also involved learning how to love my tormentors. At first, when I would pray over the people who had tormented, brutalized or abused me, I would shake with rage. Slowly, however, I surrendered my pain to God and asked Him to remove my anger. Once the anger was gone, I then asked Him to show me why He loved those who hurt me so badly. At first, admittedly, I would pray for these people purely out of obedience. After a while, though, God softened my heart and I started, miraculously, to actually love those people. I realized they had their own demons to deal with and that helped me feel compassion for them. The process began, however, when I learned how to forgive and, ultimately, to love those who did me wrong. I couldn't have done it without God's help and that of the wonderful friends He brought into my life.

"Love is patient, love is kind. It does not envy, it does not boast, it is not proud. It does not dishonor others, it is not self-seeking, it is not easily angered, it keeps no record of wrongs. Love does not delight in evil but rejoices with the truth. It always protects, always trusts, always hopes, always perseveres.
Love never fails..."
1 Corinthians 13:4-8 (NIV)

Step 7 Activity: Allowing Love In

Describe a time you felt loved.

_____

_____

_____

How did this experience make you feel?

_____

_____

Write a statement below that will help you allow love to come into your life. Post the statement where you can see it daily. I have a statement by my bathroom mirror that helps me. It says: "I am worthy of Love." Every time I go in the bathroom, I remind myself by reading it that I truly am worthy of love.

_____

_____

_____

Step 8: Learning to Love Yourself

*"She is more precious than rubies,
And all the things you may desire cannot compare
with her."*

Proverbs 3:15

I grew up in Columbus, Ohio, in a
neighborhood nicknamed "The Bottoms." The area
was run down and occupied with low-income families.
My family lived in a small two-bedroom house that
had plumbing issues upstairs. Because the upstairs
plumbing did not work, we had to shower in the
basement next to a washer and dryer with a pipe
converted to a shower. The house was never clean.
There were piles of dirt, newspapers, filthy dishes and
old, moldy clothes everywhere. If you would turn on
the light in the kitchen at night, you would see
thousands of cockroaches scatter. I would wait 30
seconds before going into the kitchen to avoid
encountering the creepy crawlies. The house was so
poorly maintained, we could not even cook in the
kitchen. Our living environment and poverty
contributed to the difficulty of caring for myself.

My sister and I used to go to The Salvation
Army camp every summer. One year my dad gave
me $10 for the canteen. Knowing that my parents had
trouble with money and our house needed many
repairs we couldn't afford, I never felt I could treat

69

myself. I went the entire week without spending the money I'd been given, so I could give it back to my dad back when the week was over. Always when I returned it, he had a look of relief on his face. So, from that moment on, I became an over-giver to the point of me sacrificing my well-being in order to help others.

This pattern continued into my adult relationships. One year, I received a bonus at work. My husband and I did not have a lot of extras so we decided to spend this money on something fun. He wanted a football jersey for $200 and I wanted a camera for about the same cost. We only had $300 to use, so I decided that he should get the jersey.

Being other-centered is a good thing, but not when it comes from a place of unworthiness in the giver's heart. When someone would give me something, I would feel guilty and stressed, then I would try to outgive them in return. My lack of self-value made me feel unworthy of gifts and rewards. I allowed others to make decisions that made them happy, even if, deep inside, they made me miserable. I even allowed my husband to buy a house I didn't like because he wanted it.

I became a self-made martyr in an attempt to feel like my presence was enough. I over-gave my talents to every organization, my time to every cause, and donated every spare dollar that I had. Deep down

I did not feel like I deserved love or even nice things. I thought I had to earn every drop of affection and kindness I received from others.

This thinking even affected my weight loss journey. I struggled with spending any resources on myself. In an effort to stay motivated, however, I decided to treat myself whenever I reached a milestone in my journey. This was a new concept for me.

Here were the rewards I gave myself along the way:

- Down 25 pounds - Get pedicure
- Down 50 pounds - Buy keyboard
- Down 75 pounds - Buy Vera Bradley backpack (For 100 pound reward)
- Down 100 pounds -Take trip to New York City
- Down 125 pounds -Trade in my truck for my dream car
- Down 150 pounds -Try indoor skydiving
- Down 175 pounds - Get massage and facial
- Down 200 pounds - Buy new outfit
- Down 212.2 pounds - Take hot air balloon ride

As I rewarded myself, I started to appreciate myself in other ways. I started loving how adventurous I was. I adored learning how to dress my changing body. I began to realize how unique God had made me. He made me passionate, funny, adventurous, caring, and most of all – His! In order for me to fall in love with myself, I had to learn to nurture and reward myself. By removing the limits I had put over my life, I learned my true worth!

"Strength and honor are her clothing;
She shall rejoice in time to come."

Proverbs 31:25

Step 8 Activity: Learning to Love Yourself

What are some things you like to do for yourself?

1. _____

2. _____

3. _____

4. _____

5. _____

How will you reward yourself along the way?

GOAL	REWARD	DATE	DONE?

HEALING THROUGH GRATITUDE

Step 9: Honoring the Past

"Jesus answered and said to him, "What I am doing you do not understand now, but you will know after this.'"

John 13:7

The time between my first and second marriage was the most shameful period of my life. I had gone from being a "good girl" who had been with only one man to a woman flirting with multiple men. I was being rebellious and fighting God. Although I was still going to church on Sunday, I was trying to find comfort in worldly pleasures. This period of my life is uncomfortable to talk about because I was the one who caused harm to myself.

Immediately after my soon to be ex-husband left, I started dating - and by dating, I mean a *lot* of dating. At one point I went on 10 different dates in a two-week span, just to feel *wanted*. Being cheated on made me feel devalued and unwanted, so I sought value from the affection of men. I did not care about my body any more. I slept with any man who gave me even the most fleeting affection and attention. I put myself in a lot of harmful situations and threw my morals completely out the window.

My first boyfriend after my marriage was a man who, after a few short months of dating, told me he was still living with his girlfriend, but he wanted to marry me. In my broken state of mind, I felt better about myself because he was choosing me over that other woman. Eventually I ended the relationship due to my guilt, but my reckless and self-loathing behavior did not stop.

At work, I pretended everything was ok, but I spent my evenings talking to strangers or "dating." On the nights that I was not consumed with attention-getting behavior, I became suicidal and tried to eat my pain away. Within a six-month period, I dated over 30 men and received multiple marriage proposals. I wore a mask of and contentment, while my careless lifestyle put me in destructive situations. Once, when I was admitted to the hospital following a suicide attempt, I had a boyfriend watch my apartment. He used the time to steal everything he could. I was devastated. In that moment, I had a decision to make: turn to God or run. I ran.

A few nights after the robbery, consumed by the seductive allure of escaping my pain, I attempted suicide again. I had plenty of medication at home that I could take, but I needed alcohol to complete the lethal cocktail. I drove to the closest convenience store I could find. There I was approached by a man who offered to buy me drinks. At first I refused his offer, but he was persistent. Eventually he paid for my drinks and walked me to my car. The details of that night are too horrifying to recount here, but they shaped my future. I became a rape statistic.

Immediately following the assault, I went home and did everything you're not supposed to do in such a situation. I showered, brushed my teeth, and washed my clothes. Many times. But I could not get the dirty feeling off of me. I cried hysterically until I could not think any more and wondered why I had to endure so much misery. I wanted to be out of this world and stop hurting all the time.

A friend of mine called the police when I did not answer the phone, and I was taken to the emergency room for examination. When I was asked if I wanted to press charges, I declined. I did not want to go through the horror of a trial. The guilt and shame of not pressing charges weighed on me heavily for years to come. "What if he did this to another woman?" I worried over and over again. "What if he hurt her more than he had me? Why didn't I value myself? Why does everyone who hurt me get away with what they did?"

This rabbit trail of thoughts was preventing me from moving forward. I was stuck in the past and the bad decisions I had repeatedly made haunted me. I fixated on the bad, rather than focusing on the potential I had to change.

Trusting God helped me figure out that I needed to take inventory of my life. I sat down and reviewed-every tragic event I went through, deciding to focus on the lessons I learned from them. I made a list of what they were:

- I realized that I was strong because I survived the horror of having my sexuality used against me.
- I learned I was a person of value, that I needed to allow God to fill the void inside me.
- I learned the importance and benefits of being vulnerable, forgave the other woman for the pain she caused me and, eventually, to forgive myself for the pain I caused others.

This list took time and prayer to compile, but I am glad I did because now I am thankful for the lessons. This practice also helped me remove any guilt and shame I was feeling.

Step 9 Activity: Honoring the Past

Write down events that have impacted you and what you have learned from them. Take more room if needed. Take your time on this.

EVENT	LESSON

Take a moment to pray and thank God for the lessons learned.

Step 10: Honoring Yourself

"Rejoice always, pray without ceasing, in everything give thanks; for this is the will of God in Christ Jesus for you."

1 Thessalonians 5:16-18

As a little girl, I loved to paint and be creative. In first grade I painted a dog with lots different colored limbs, polka dots, and flowers. It received an award and was featured in a display at the Ohio State Fair.

Until this happened, my teachers thought I was mentally delayed. I rarely spoke and had a huge speech impediment. When they saw I had this special talent, however, they decided to give me a test. The results showed that I actually belonged in the "Gifted and Talented" program, not at a table with children who had special needs.

My dad was excited when he saw me win awards, though he did encourage me to focus on academic success, rather than artistic talent. Though I loved art, making my dad happy was even more important. This made me work hard to win awards. If I wasn't the best at whatever I tried, I became deeply critical of myself. Eventually, I lost touch with who I was and what was important to me, focusing more on what got me approval than what truly made me happy.

My father loved The Ohio State University so, because I wanted to make him happy, I went to that college though I had scholarships elsewhere. My attempts to please Daddy even led me to earn a Master's degree in Business Administration with a 3.7 GPA. Keep in mind, I did this while also working full time. Still, I never felt it was good enough because I hadn't gotten a 4.0. I wanted to be perfect.

This pattern of craving praise followed me for many years. I worked hard at whatever I did just to fulfill my need for affection. I became a chameleon, changing who I was to suit those I was with at the time. My dad loved politics, so I studied politics. I became obsessed with football because my first husband loved football. I obsessively watched Anime©® programs, though I didn't like them, simply because my second husband loved them. I wanted to support those around me and was willing to stifle myself completely to do so.

Not surprisingly, when God began delivering me and setting me free, I discovered that I no longer knew who I was or what I liked . My entire life had been lived for everyone else. If I wanted to be whole again and shed the weight I'd carried, both physically and emotionally, for a very long time, I would have to come into touch with who I was.

My first step was to start painting again. (I'd always had a passion for art and it had been very painful to lay it aside back in high school.) To my shock people loved my paintings and started buying them!

I then wondered what else I had stopped doing that had given me satisfaction. I quickly recalled that I loved to sing and perform. Due to my poor self-perception, however, I struggled to get back on the stage. Eventually, though, I gained enough courage to join the worship team at church.

I started singing behind the piano. Then, through the encouragement of the worship director at my church, I eventually sang a small solo. Like a tiny seedling, my confidence sprouted and began to grow, and I started going out to events and talking to people.

After a while, I became confident enough to risk trying new things, all in pursuit of finding out what else would give me join. I travelled to New York, Ohio, and Arizona on my own and discovered a love for travel. I also learned that I loved to hike, do graphic design, and organize events. I started honoring and even celebrating who I was, and, if I did not like something, I chose to walk away. I no longer apologized for who I was.

Eventually I had the opportunity to participate in a weekly discussion group with people of diverse religious beliefs. At first, I struggled with speaking up and saying what I believed because I wanted everyone to like me. As time went by, however, I realized that God had placed me in this group to learn to stand for my beliefs.

I started reading The Word every chance I could and researched the Bible to understand why I believed the way I did. Through challenging my faith and bravely speaking about what I believed with people who thought differently, I grew in confidence and strength in my faith. This helped me start to honor myself in other areas of my life, including the way I treated my body.

Why did I dishonor my body? (That's of course what I was doing when I stuffed it rather than nourishing it in a healthy manner.) Because I did not know any better. Once God helped me realize and rejoice in how uniquely I was made. I started to love all that made me who I was: a woman who loved God, the Bible, prayer, glitter, and elephants; had a huge sense of humor, was snarky, blunt, and loved to excel; is a cheerleader, strives on organization, and most importantly, is not perfect. After I stopped apologizing for who I was and embraced the qualities God had given me, I learned I did not have to hide behind my body. I was "fearfully and wonderfully made!" (Psalm 139:14, NKJV)

Be-YOU-tiful

Step 10 Activity: Honoring Yourself

List some qualities about yourself that make you unique. What do you love about yourself?

1. _____

2. _____

3. _____

4. _____

5. _____

Fill in the blanks, using your unique traits, as you've listed them above:

God has designed me to be unique. I am beautifully

made because of _____,

_____, _____,

_____, and _____.

I am thankful for who the Lord has made me to be.

Step 11: The Gift of Deeper Gratitude

"I thank my God upon every remembrance of you...."
Philippians 1:3

On my 29th birthday I married my second husband. At the time the idea seemed so perfect. Birthdays of my past were nothing more than bad memories. Now I believed they would get better. We'd even gotten engaged on his birthday! After he blew out the candles on the cake I'd baked him, he told me what he'd wished: that I would be his wife.

When we discussed the wedding date, he commented, "Since you have had bad experiences on your birthday, let's make a good memory and get married on your birthday." We eloped that year and I had such a joyful memory on my birthday. I never thought that we would break up or that this event would cause deeper pain with an annual reminder.

The first anniversary after my husband left, I was dismayed. I wondered how I would survive the day. Not only had he moved across the country without a good-bye; he'd actually left with his *girlfriend*, a married coworker that I thought was my friend. It was a dual betrayal and I felt like a fool.

All I wanted to do on that birthday was eat pizza, binge-watch TV, and cry. Fortunately God had other ideas for me, ones that would teach me a lesson about gratitude and choosing to be happy in any circumstance.

Two nights before my birthday, I prayed, asking God to show me how to get through that special day. His response struck me as a little bit crazy: "P*aint 12 postcards and put Romans 12:12 on the back of each one."* Then he told me to pass these 12 postcards out to strangers on my birthday.

Though I was baffled by His instructions, I decided to obey. The evening before my birthday, I decorated 12 cards with angels, crosses, flowers, and forest scenery. On the back, I wrote *Romans 12:12: "Be joyful in hope, patient in tribulation, and faithful in prayer."*

The next morning when I awoke, I was seized with what can only be described as pure terror. I was petrified about going up to strangers and handing them a gift. Still I was obedient and took the cards out around town. My first stop was Walgreens where I gave one of my cards to a man who was waiting for a prescription. He was shocked but loved hearing that I was giving them out to people as a way to celebrate my birthday. Then I said a prayer for him and went on my way.

My entire body was shaking as I left this interaction, but I continued to press forward. At first I felt stupid but, as the day continued, I realized God was showing me that, even on a day as bleak as my birthday had become for me, I could give back to others and bring light into the world. What's more, I brought the some joy and happiness to myself.

That same day I gave a lady who could barely walk a ride home. The angel postcard I gave her, she told me, was a "sign from God" that her mom was in heaven because the angel looked just like her dear departed mother.

I gave another card to a barista at a coffee stand I frequented, when she told me that she and her boyfriend had been fighting. It seemed like she needed the encouragement.

Another lady told me that she was starting to lose faith in God but receiving the card from me was a sign to her that "God saw me."

What had originally seemed like a "crazy act" had been transformed by God into a wellspring of gratitude for others and for life. Yes, my life was in pieces, but there was hope if I allowed God to work through me in spite of how I felt.

Later that month I found a live-streaming application called Periscope. Through God's direction

I began broadcasting my own simple Bible-based program there on a regular basis. In my sorrow I had experienced a deeper gratitude and love for others that had given me the confidence necessary to try a more public form of encouragement.

At first, I hated the way I looked on my broadcasts. I did not have a neck, my face was fat, I had a triple-chin, et cetera. By broadcasting and helping people even when I was in such an unhappy place, however, I grew more confident in myself and found people who loved and cared for me. Of course there were some viewers who made fun of me, but I learned that these people were also hurting, and this gave me an opportunity to love them and be thankful for them, just as I had longed to be loved and appreciated for many years myself.

I have learned that, in our pain, we must find gratitude for the good in our life. Often that starts by serving others. By serving like Jesus served when He washed His disciples' feet of the disciples, I was able to climb out of my negative emotions and find a joy in living. Giving back to others helped me see and appreciate all the blessings I had in my life. Now, when I am feeling stuck in my emotions, I reach out to help others and be a light to this world.

"Only a life lived in the service of others is worth living."

Albert Einstein

Day 11 Activity: The Gift of Deeper Gratitude

What are some activities you can do to help you move past your sorrows and bring hope and joy to others?

_____

_____

_____

_____

_____

Now, make a promise to use these tools when you are feeling sad or hopeless:

I will _____ every
_____.

EXTENDING FORGIVENESS

Step 12: Dealing with Offenders

"...love your enemies, bless those who curse you, do good to those who hate you, and pray for those who spitefully use you and persecute you...."

Matthew 5:44

If you don't already know it by now, I was definitely a daddy's girl. Wherever my dad was, that's where I wanted to be. My dad loved going to local sporting events, being active in the community and in politics. Since he was always nicer to me than my mom, I thought he could do no wrong. It was therefore a big shock when I learned, many years later after his death, that he had actually been a big offender/abuser in my life.

The signs of who he really was were there all along, of course. The Monday before the Saturday I wed for the first time, for example, I got a call from my father's husband that my dad was missing. I stopped all my wedding preparation to go look for him. We called the hospitals and police stations. Four hours later we learned that my dad was in the jail, having been arrested for indecent exposure at a local park. The cops told us he would be there for a week. Consequently he would not be able to attend my wedding. Thankfully my grandfather agreed to walk me down the aisle and, though I loved having my grandfather do the honors, I really wanted my dad to be the one to give me away.

An hour before the ceremony, my father showed up for the wedding, forcing me to tell him that my grandfather had taken his place. I could not take that honor away from my grandfather now, I explained. Then I asked my dad why he had chosen to get himself in trouble right then, just before the biggest day of my life. He was stressed out about me getting married, he told me, and wanted to forget his problems. Again I was the reason for the dysfunction.

A second piece of evidence arose while I was in elementary school. Back then my father "had to go away for a weekend," I was told, because he got caught "peeing in the park."

My dad also got beat up for, it was said, "trying to help get a pregnant woman to the hospital."

Sadly, because I put my dad on such a high pedestal, I could not see the writing on the wall. It was not until my wedding day that the depths of the lies my parents told us to hide his alternative lifestyle really sunk in. The day I found out my dad was homosexual, I felt like my entire existence was a lie. Only then did the clues of who he really was start to line up.

Life was never the same after that moment. My father embraced his new lifestyle, even at the expense of hurting me, to proclaim he was homosexual. In my senior year of high school, he placed an ad in the football program to honor his graduating daughter. He didn't just say, "Congratulations, Beckie!" however. Instead he chose to post a picture of himself and his partner in the ad, signing it "Your Two Dads." I'd only met his partner once before the ad came out.

Even when I realized how much my parents had lied to me, I didn't really know how much abuse my father had caused in my life until I was at his funeral. I saw how fragile he looked. When he was alive I had always tried to make excuses for him. There was always a reason I found for him not taking my sister and I out of an abusive home, keeping the house dirty, or not taking adequate care for our health. I was so desperate for my dad's approval and love that I overlooked all those things, as well as his unfaithfulness to my mom and not standing up for us when she abused us.

As I was going through the healing process, however, I had to face reality. No longer could I make excuses for his behavior or anyone else's. By justifying others' actions, I was not facing the pain or hurt I felt. This caused me to stuff the pain down deep inside. Then I would eat my pain away.

One day I decided to write down every offender that had ever been in my life, big and small. In order to heal I had to know what was hidden deep inside. My list not only included my father who I adored but old classmates who teased me, co-workers, pastors, neighbors, friends, et cetera. There was no need to confront these people because a lot of them were in my distant memory but I needed to acknowledge how they offended me so I could eventually heal that wound.

"Forgiveness does not change the past but it does enlarge the future."

-- Paul Lewis Boese

Step 12 Activity: Dealing with Offenders

Identify the major offenders in your life. List them below:

PERSON	EVENT

How can you love them?

PERSON	How can I love them?

Step 13: Releasing Forgiveness

"…bearing with one another, and forgiving one another, if anyone has a complaint against another; even as Christ forgave you, so you also must do."

Colossians 3:13

In September 2016, nearly a year after I found out my second husband had moved to Georgia, I took a class that helped me explore my emotions. One of the tasks was to write forgiveness letters. Being the over-achiever I am, I quickly took to this task. I did not realize how difficult writing forgiveness letters would be until I started.

One day I packed my lunch and went down to a local beach on the Puget Sound. I sat looking at the water praying and writing. Using a list I'd drawn up of the biggest offenders in my life, I started writing. The letters would never be seen by the offender. Their purpose was to give me an opportunity to release the pain, not confront the offending party. As I wrote the letters, I could not stop crying. (Thankfully I had sunglasses on so I could cry freely as I wrote without drawing attention.)

In each letter I was instructed to include why I was grateful for the person who had hurt me. The most difficult people to be grateful for and, in so doing, forgive were the people I did not know: the woman my first husband had an affair with and the man who sexually assaulted me. At points when I was writing, I would shake with anger, disgust and brokenness. How could I possibly be grateful for a person who stole my husband and another who hurt me without remorse? What was good in them? How could I love them? Why did I need to love them, let alone forgive them?

I chose to begin with the woman who had the affair with my first husband. We'd actually had a few conversations online discussing him, soon after I learned of his relationship with her. She was under the belief that my husband and I were just living together for financial reasons. That was news to me. When I asked her to back off, she did not. I carried a ton of envy and jealousy of her; "Why did he choose her?" I often asked myself. "What made her better than me?" The problem wasn't her, really; it was the hatred I had in my heart for myself.

For years I had judged myself against others instead of finding my own identity. I now realized that I would have to write *myself* a forgiveness letter as I was the biggest offender of my life. I decided to write myself a letter forgiving myself and made a vow to treat myself better. I soon realized, however, that it would take more months of reprogramming my brain to fully complete the process. (I'll talk more about that in later chapters.)

100

Eventually I was able to find ways to love the other woman. She loved my ex-husband and she helped me see that he was not the right person for me.

When I began trying to write a letter to the person who sexually assaulted me, I was again at a loss to find any understanding and compassion. "What could make someone so evil? Does forgiving him justify the act he committed? Will he ever understand the damage of what he did?"

Though the questions I had were understandable, they were also preventing me from releasing forgiveness for him. As long as those questions, which actually stemmed from anger and hurt, stood between me and that man, I would not be able to see him through the eyes of God.

As soon as I realized this, I prayed to see the man as God saw him. I asked God to reveal his heart to me so I could grant forgiveness. God showed me that the man had been severely hurt in his past and was still living in pain. He was so consumed with this world, God furthermore explained that he did not think what he was doing was damaging. Suddenly I could see my abuser with love and compassion and I was thankful for his life. Now he is on my daily prayer list.

There are still times that I get consumed with grief and get angry with the people who hurt me. At times I will allow myself to have a moment of pain but I put a time limit on the grief. I carry the letters in my vehicle for those rare times I cannot get out of my own mind. I look at the notebook (not the letter) and remember I already forgave the offenders. The letters remind me that I let go of the pain they caused me and they have no control over me any more.

In writing the letters, some other things became clear to me. I had held onto the pain because I wanted to bring justice to the situation but hating them had only caused me to become more hateful towards myself. When I found ways to love and forgive those who hurt and abused me, however, I also found I could love and forgive myself.

Writing forgiveness letters does not justify the actions a wrongdoer has committed against us, but it does provide us with a way to release our pain. Moreover, holding onto hurt and pain never really punishes someone for the pain they caused us, but it does prevent us from being free.

"But I tell you, love your enemies and pray for those who persecute you"

Matthew 5:44

Step 13 Activity: Releasing Forgiveness

Write a forgiveness letter to every person who has offended you. This could take some time and it will, no doubt, be a difficult process. Include in each letter:

- The situation that caused you pain or abuse
- The emotions which are tied to this situation
- An apology for your part in the conflict
- The things you learned from this experience
- Specific reasons you are thankful for them

When you are finished writing your letter, forgive the offender and release the pain to God. Here is an example of a letter I wrote to my mom:

Mom,

I was hurt when you hit me and called me names. I felt as if you did not love me because you did not take care of us and you let the house overfill with filth. I am angry I felt so unloved by you. I am sorry if my presence annoyed you I just wanted to be loved. I deserved to have a mother that loved me. I am sad that I did not to get to know you better before you died. I heard you had a funny sense of humor and I never got to see that. I learned so much from you. The neglect, abuse, and harmful words taught me how not to live. I forgive you for all the pain. I release any shame and hurt I feel. You are entirely forgiven.

Beckie

Keep the letters for reference when you start to feel the pain of the past overwhelming you. *Never mail them to the offender! This exercise is for your benefit alone!*

"Forgive others, not because they deserve forgiveness,
but because you deserve peace."

Jonathan Lockwood Huie, Author

Step 14: Gaining Gratitude for Offenses

"No one has seen God at any time. If we love one another, God abides in us, and His love has been perfected in us."

1 John 4:12

In Step 9 we learned that, to honor the past, we must practice gratitude. The events you have encountered in your life have shaped you into the person you have become. Be thankful for them. God has a plan to cause all things, even the worst of them, to work together for your good. Secondly, who you are currently is beautiful, whether you believe that to be true right now or not. Finally, take confidence in knowing that you have survived the worst day of your life. No matter what has happened in your life, you have survived, and that, in itself, is victorious.

I once had a habit of thinking that I was not living a victorious and abundant life because I had not yet become the person I wanted to be. This made me lose sight of the fact that I was exactly where I needed to be. Over time I learned to stop comparing my life in comparison to how close I'd come to fulfilling my dreams. Instead, I chose to start loving the path I was on right then and enjoying that journey, day by day.

Yes, I have gone through a lot of hell in my life but, not only did I conquer the battle, I came out better! I can now look back at all the trials, heartache, and betrayal I've gone through and be grateful for it. Within those difficulties were life lessons that shaped me into the woman I am today and enabled me to encourage others that they can make it, too!

You can say the same thing about your life, too! You can find a piece of joy within any trial you've gone through, even if it's only to say, "I survived." What's more, every bad situation or circumstance has a lesson in it that will help you learn and grow into the person you long to be. I learned to love people like Jesus and to see them through Christ's love.

Every single bad thing that has happened to you has shaped you into the person you are today, and that person has something beneficial to give back to the world.

Growing up with an abusive mom was difficult. Often I found myself wishing my mom was not around. Trying to write a forgiveness letter to her was hard. I couldn't find a single thing I was thankful for about her.

On my first day of school, my mom was overly stressed so she yelled at me the entire time I was getting ready. That day, I was wearing a dress that had a matching purse. Just before I had to leave for the bus stop, I could not find my purse. My mom became infuriated and started cussing. The nasty words escalated quickly to hitting. Then, in her fury, she threw me down the stairs.

Luckily I was not hurt, except for a few bruises, and I found my purse sitting next to the toilet. My mom walked me to the bus stop, telling me she loved me as she loaded me onto the bus. Back then I didn't even realize her abusive behavior was abnormal.

At my school, each of our buses was coded with a different colored sign. The bus I needed to take home was the one with a green sign but when my teacher asked "What color bus do you take home," I misunderstood and told them the color of the bus, not the color of the sign on it. As a result, I was placed on the yellow bus. When I did not recognize where we were, I was relieved. I knew I wasn't home and that was good enough for me. Eventually, after all the other kids were dropped off, the bus driver noticed I was still there, figured out where I was supposed to go and took me home.

My mother was standing at the bus stop, sobbing, when I arrived. She hugged me with relief as I climbed off the bus but, as soon as we got in the house, I was cussed out for being dumb and beaten yet again. I never understood why my mom be was "perfect" in public but, behind closed doors, she tortured me. The years of abuse continued with too many stories to tell but the reason for every one of them was rooted in my mom's own inner pain and suffering, which she projected on my sister and myself.

I did not understand my mother's mental health issues until after I moved out of her house. They became clear, however, the weekend I first got married.

I was getting ready for my wedding, so my mom decided she wanted to drive back to Ohio from Tennessee to be there for me. Her eyesight was very poor, however, so she had her second husband drive her there.

While in Ohio, she needed to go to the store. Her husband was too tired to drive her there so I took her where she needed to go. (My own eyesight was pretty bad, but still good enough to drive.)

That trip gave us the chance to talk about the abuse for the first time in our lives. She was even the one to bring the subject up. "I am so sorry, Rebecca, for everything," she said through free flowing tears. "Whenever I hurt you I was not meaning to hurt you; I just saw red." She had suffered from a lot of abuse when she was growing up, too, she told me, and she was overly stressed with being married to my father. Slowly, she poured out her heart to me about everything. Suddenly, I no longer was the woman who had beaten me; instead, I saw a broken person trying to heal. I could see her with Christ's eyes and she was beautiful. Unfortunately, only a couple years later, she would die in a car accident before our relationship could be fully recovered.

At her funeral I was able to see my mom through other people's eyes. I heard that my mom was funny and often talked about her girls. I heard how proud she was that I was in college and driving. I saw her at home with her new husband. It was clean and orderly, not in shambles like the house we had. I could not hold on to my pain any more. I had to learn to love my mom through the pain. Without her in my life, I would not be where I am today. How difficult it must have been for her to live with a husband that was cheating on her with other men, all while she also suffered with eyesight and weight problems and our family struggled to get by on a very tiny income.

Sometimes we are so focused on the pain others have caused us that we forget to look at the entire picture and the pain our abusers are in. When Christ was on the cross, He was in pain but he put his pain aside and focused on the suffering of those He died to save.

Honor your pain because it is valid but learn to look at the event in its entirety. Only then will you be able to find the compassion you need to fully release those who've abused you and let forgiveness flow. Today, I have gratitude that I learned how to be strong and a survivor from my mom. Once you learn to have gratitude for the situations you've endured, then you will be able to heal, also.

"Jesus said, "Father, forgive them, for they do not know what they are doing."

Luke 23:24

Step 14 Activity: Gaining Gratitude for the Offense

What lessons have you learned from your past?

_____

_____

_____

_____

_____

How can you mentor people because of what you've suffered?

_____

_____

_____

_____

Say a prayer to thank God for carrying you through.

Step 15: Establishing Healthy Boundaries

*"Keep your heart with all diligence,
for out of it spring the issues of life."*

Proverbs 4:23

My entire life I just wanted to please people. At times this idea cost me money and heartbreak. Growing up as the peacemaker in my house, I always bent over backwards to make people feel valued and loved. I continually gave more than I had: time, emotions, money, and energy. I couldn't tell people "No" because I did not want them to feel let down. Not having boundaries caused me to mask my pain and eat more so I knew I had to address this in order to lose weight.

My second husband showed me how loose my boundaries were. I would never cuss in front of him, smoke weed, party, and I allowed the bad treatment he gave me. Sometimes he would change plans at the last minute or not come home at all, and never offer a reason why. If I questioned him, I was told I was crazy and overreacting. I learned to allow behaviors that were unacceptable just to appease him.

I wanted to make my marriage work with him, so I tried to change to be like him. I even took up drinking and smoking marijuana. After a while, I even gave up trying to serve God, simply because I was so depressed and felt I'd let Him down.

113

The New Year's Eve before he left, my husband told me he had to do inventory in one of his stores located far away. He took me to dinner, then said he would come home after midnight. I was devastated and offered to drive him to the store just so we could be together.

Midnight came and went and, still, he was not home. In fact, he didn't come home at all that evening. As for me, I didn't sleep a wink because I was on the phone all night, frantically calling the police and hospitals to see if I could find him.

When he finally came home at 11 A.M. the next morning, I did not care what his story was. I was just glad he was home, safe and sound. He, on the other hand, was angry with me for calling his coworkers to find out if he was okay. I apologized and felt bad for "being crazy." Later, however, I learned he had not been at work at all, but had attended a party with the same lady he left me for a month later.

I ignored the sexting messages and pictures of himself I later found on his phone. I ignored it when he started coming home late every night and taking a shower once he got in. Instead, I turned the blame for his behavior on myself. "If only I loved him better, he would come to his senses," I told myself. No matter how many times I turned the other cheek and tried to love him more, however, our relationship did not improve. My husband still left And I was left, yet again, having given

114

all I could to my partner, only to end up being used up, abused, and alone.

For a while, after he moved out, we continued to date. I accepted the fact that he sometimes did not call or message me for days on end. Whenever he did call, I would drop everything and take the call. I tried everything to win him back with love. I even willingly sacrificed my self-worth in an effort to help him.

New York Times bestselling romance writer Penny Reid once penned this pithy and wise statement: "Stop setting yourself on fire in order to keep the other person warm." Sadly, that's exactly what I had been doing, time and time again, in an effort to make my second husband happy. I wasn't happy, of course, but I thought my happiness did not matter.

This behavior carried on for two-and-a-half years before I learned that I was worth more. As I walked to the courthouse to file for divorce, I was scared. I had never said "No" to anyone. Although he had left the marriage, he was still texting me, saying he'd made a mistake and wanted to get back together with me. Once he even asked me to move to Georgia with him and not mention his unfaithfulness and abuse again. For a while, I actually thought about honoring his request because I had been praying for my marriage to be restored. Eventually, however, I saw that his actions were not matching his words.

As I walked into the courthouse, I received a message from someone who did not know I was filing that day. The note said that God was ok with me moving forward with this process. In that moment, I realized that forgiveness did not mean that we should let people walk all over us. Rather, it is ok to set boundaries and say that a person's treatment of you is not okay. It is okay to stand up for yourself.

Today, I always set boundaries in my life and tell people "No" when I need to do so. Being a woman and a natural people pleaser, I have to remind myself of my priorities, from time to time, as well as continue to assess if a person's treatment of me is worth enduring. Sometimes, I can find a way to deal with their behavior, but if I can't, I give myself permission to exit or otherwise stay clear of the individual. Setting clear boundaries in your life is not a punishment yet an opportunity for you to develop healthy long lasting relationships.

" 'No' is a complete sentence!"

-- Author Unknown

Step 15 Activity: Establishing Healthy Boundaries

A lot of people with weight issues have codependency issues also and will say "Yes" to anything someone asks of you. Now hear this: you are allowed to say "No." In fact, learning how and when to draw the line will save you from many future traumas.

You deserve to have a normal, healthy life with friends who truly love and respect you. Yes, you are worth it. Today, right now, let's set some boundaries that will help save you from destructive relationships. It's time to scream, "NO!"

In what areas of your life do you need to set boundaries?

_____

_____

_____

_____

_____

Make a plan that includes:

- **A set of ground rules**
- **A plan for communicating those rules to others**
- **A way of enforcing the rules**

What is your plan?

_____

_____

_____

_____

_____

_____

EMBRACING YOUR NEW IDENTITY

Step 16: Identify Your Weaknesses

"Examine yourselves as to whether you are in the faith. Test yourselves. Do you not know yourselves, that Jesus Christ is in you—unless indeed you are disqualified?'

2 Corinthians 13:5

I was born with congenital cataracts causing extreme eyesight issues. When I was a baby, they took the lenses out of my eyes, causing my eyesight to be blurred when my glasses were off. Even with my glasses on, I could barely see out of my left eye. I had to work twice as hard to read and sit close to the front of the classroom. When I took my glasses off, I was barely able to walk a few feet due to the lack of clarity. I did not let this stop me.

I loved to swim so I would be in a pool as often as possible during the summer. I wasn't allowed to swim with my glasses on, for fear the expensive eyewear would get broken or lost. For that reason, I usually put my glasses on my beach towel, then carefully made my way to the pool, putting one foot in front of the other, being intentional with every step.

Once I was in the pool, I had to count how many strokes it was from side to side so I wouldn't bump my head on the wall due to problems with my depth perception. Playing pool games was, of course, difficult.

Even with these disadvantages, I worked two years at an apartment pool to help my mom pay bills. I knew my eyesight was a hindrance in the water so I found ways to embrace the difference. I would swim longer hours and learn to hold my breath longer to give myself more time to find hidden objects at the bottom of the pool.

In elementary school I loved to dance, cheerlead, and do gymnastics. I would practice any chance I got and enjoyed performing. Due to my parents' lack of feeding us girls properly, often I could not keep up or became lethargic. For as far back as I could remember, I was always the "big" girl and I was always chosen last for sports. Still, I remained active in gymnastics and cheerleading until I wasn't chosen for the teams because my body was not a fit. My body was my weakness because I couldn't perform the routines the way the smaller girls could. Eventually, I gave up trying to perform in those sports because I felt I was weak.

I also discovered that I had weaknesses other people did not suffer with. Because of the abuse I suffered at home, I couldn't take criticism well and became a perfectionist. This was damaging to my career and self-esteem. I had a nervous breakdown in front of the director at a bank where I worked because I could not receive his constructive feedback. I knew I had to face what was wrong with me if I was ever to conquer the problems I had with my weight. Those were the issues that led me to be depressed and overeat.

Not surprisingly, my obesity made me loathe looking at myself in the mirror. Any chance I got to avoid a mirror, I would. In an effort to avoid staring at myself, I would not do my makeup or hair. When I did catch a glimpse of myself, I could only think of how I had let myself go and how ugly I was.

This pattern continued for years. Any picture of myself was deleted and I forced people to take only head shots of me. Then came that day I became brave and started broadcasting on a live video feed called Periscope©®.

Here I was broadcasting to the world while staring at myself. As I did so, tapes would play in my head about how small my teeth were, how narrow my eyes were, and look how fat and ugly I was. Despite all the pain this caused, I kept going because God told me to do so. I did receive negative comments about myself that hurt but, somehow God helped me use them to make me stronger.

Finally, the day came that I wanted to conquer the demons in my head for good. Standing in my bedroom alone, I took off all my clothes and stared at my reflection in front of a full length mirror. There I was, with all my curves, scars and imperfections staring back at me. As I stood there, I faced all the bad about myself, both physically and mentally. At first I felt so much shame about how far I'd let myself go. I was a wreck in both body and mind. After about 10 minutes of beating myself up and facing all of my imperfections, I started to just see shapes.

Facing myself boldly like that was necessary. If I ever wanted to know where I was going, I first had to find out where I stood right now. What exactly were my weaknesses so I could make them strengths?

In that moment my weaknesses were fairly basic. I had trouble walking and keeping my emotional composure. I decided to start walking on a regular basis. Walking helped me deal with my emotions as well as my physical weakness.

As I faced and began to work on these issues, I discovered something very important that still helps me today: Acknowledgment of weakness does not mean you're caving into defeat; it means owning who you are in that moment and making a commitment to do better.

"You are strong when you know your weaknesses. You are beautiful when you appreciate your flaws. You are wise when you learn from your mistakes."

--Anil Sinha, Police Officer, India

Step 16 Activity: Identify Your Weaknesses

We all have things that we could improve. List a few of your needed areas of improvement below:

1. _____

2. _____

3. _____

4. _____

5. _____

How do these weaknesses impact your life?

_____

_____

_____

Step 17: Identify Your Strengths

"...casting down arguments and every high thing that exalts itself against the knowledge of God, bringing every thought into captivity to the obedience of Christ...."

2 Corinthians 10:5

My family attended the Salvation Army church in Columbus, OH, when I was in elementary school. I was a Sunbeam, which was the denomination's equivalent to a Girl Scout. During one of our meetings, we were asked to list things we loved about ourselves: what made us unique, what made us beautiful?

I listened as each of the ten other Sunbeams spouted out all the things they loved about themselves. Some loved their physical beauty. Others mentioned various talents they possessed. I sat there amazed at how easily they could talk highly about themselves. When my turn came, I couldn't think of a single thing I liked about myself. The leader tried to help. "Do you like your hair? How about your intelligence? What about your personality?" To everything I answered, "No." Finally I said I liked my eyebrows.

Even that, of course, was a stretch for me. My entire life, all I had ever heard about myself was negative. I was ugly, fat, lazy, and stupid. Sadly, because of all the traumatic I'd experienced as a child, I

125

believed all those lies. Moreover I was terrified that everything my mom said about me was right. I believed everyone saw only negative things in me. That's why I was picked last at sports. That's why I did not get asked out. That's why I wasn't chosen for special assignments at school.

Then, when I was in fifth grade, my mindset began to shift, all thanks to my teacher, Ms. Durrell. Ms. Durrell was young, hip, smart, and pretty. She even played basketball! She was everything I wanted to be.

Ms. Durrell seemed to like me and pushed me to go the extra mile. When I achieved that, she would encourage me to push myself more.

Each year, our school had a science/health fair. Ms. Durrell encouraged me to participate by talking to visitors about my eye condition. Prior to that moment, I had always tried to hide this disability as best as I could, even though anyone could tell I had vision problems, just by looking at the thick glasses on my face.

When, after bravely following through on my teacher's suggestion, I won the first place ribbon at the fair, I could not believe it. Ms. Durrell seemed even more excited than I was. She continued her support when we had to discuss Black History Heroes and make a presentation to the class about an African American icon we admired.

Ms. Durrell suggested I talk about Aretha Franklin. She even loaned me her cassette of Aretha Franklin music so I could become more acquainted with her. I did more than play the tape. When the time came for me to present, I surprised everyone, including Mrs. Durrell, by singing along with that tape and dancing to Aretha's famous song, "R-E-S-P-E-C-T." When I finished, the entire classroom erupted into cheers and high fived me. I went from a silent student, hardly noticed from day to day, to one with an outgoing personality, all due to Mrs. Durrell's encouragement.

Even when I failed, my teacher continued to encourage me. Once, our school was having field day during which students would participate in various athletic contests. Unaware of the lack of nutrition my body was receiving because I was being poorly fed at home, Ms. Durrell signed me up for the mile run. I performed horribly in the race. Not only did I finish last; I finished after the 4th graders who started five minutes after we did. I was so embarrassed! Still, at the end of the race, Ms. Durrell, noticing the tears running down my face, greeted me with a hug. Then she had the entire class give me high fives. She was proud of me, she said, because I did not quit. She loved my determination. In that moment, Ms. Durrell taught me that what I thought about myself was wrong; someone did believe in me.

I continued to come out of my shell in the years to come. While still in high school, I won a Hixson Award from the Kiwanis Club for my many hours of community service, and received scholarships that helped me pay for college. Later, after high school graduation, I was named employee of the year at two of the companies I worked for, received my Bachelor of Science in Business Management and my MBA, and became financially independent. I really wasn't the failure and mess I thought I was.

Since then, I have learned to look not only at the weaknesses in myself but to examine my strengths, as well. No matter what happens, I will not quit or give up. I am always encouraging and loving people. I believe the best in people. I am intelligent and actually quite cute. My life experiences have made me relatable to everyone. I am funny and I have a heart of gold.

If you struggle with finding strength or good attributes in yourself, ask others for their opinions. Oftentimes the things we think are faults or weakness are perceived quite positively by others. I needed Ms. Durrell to show me who I really was and not what I thought I was. She helped me find the strength within myself.

"Life is tough, my darling, but so are you."

-- Stephanie Bennett Henry, Poet

Step 17 Activity: Identify Your Strengths

List your strengths:

1. _____
2. _____
3. _____
4. _____
5. _____

How can you use these strengths to accomplish your goal?

_____

_____

_____

Step 18: Discovering Who You Really Are

"Death and life are in the power of the tongue, And those who love it will eat its fruit."

Proverbs 18:21

"Call me Beckie," sounds innocent enough. What you don't hear, however, is the constant harassment I got from this phrase.

When I was in 9th grade, a teacher was taking attendance the first day of school. "When I call your name, if you have a nickname," she asked, "go ahead and tell me."

"Call me Beckie," I replied when she finally came to me. Not thinking anything of what I said, another student mimicked me, repeating what I'd said very slowly, making me sound as if I were mentally delayed. From that day forward, kids would make fun of my name and repeat that phrase, exactly as the other student had said it. The harassment continued until I finally stood up for myself.

After this incident I disliked my name and was afraid to say who I was. Besides the tapes that played in my head about how lazy, fat, ugly, and dumb I was, now I couldn't even say my name without feeling somehow deficient. My entire identity was shattered. I gave people control over me with their words, not realizing that I had the power to either accept what they said or stand firm in knowing who I really was.

Shortly after my second husband left me, I sat in a local coffee shop asking God, Who am I?" My entire life I had tried to fit into everyone's picture of who I was, not who I truly felt I was. In that moment I heard God say, Look up your name." First, I looked up Rebecca. It meant "servant of God." I then looked up my middle name, Renea. That meant "Beautiful of having love." Finally, I looked up Ryan. This meant "little king/leader." Right there in that public place, I began to cry. I was Rebecca Renea Ryan, servant of God, beautiful of having love, a leader. WOW!

God does not see us the way the world does. He has made us perfect and unique. All my life, I had hidden how unique I was because I was afraid of being teased. Right up until that moment in the coffee shop, all my "I am" statements, the words that described how I saw myself, were negative. Even more importantly, they did not reflect who God created me to be.

Suddenly I realized that, up until that very moment, in my despair and brokenness, I had questioned who I was. Though I had devoted every free moment to reading my bible, I had done so through a lens that saw God was judging me. My imperfections made me believe I was unworthy of love, both God's and other people's. As a result, I poured all my efforts into earning that love. How wrong I had been! God saw me as deserving of His love, a servant leader who also deserved the love of other people.

With the help of friends, I started to reprogram my brain. I wrote down 10 "I am" statements to help change my thinking: I am loved, worthy, strong, enough, beautiful, intelligent, highly favored, brave, creative, and created for a purpose. I began speaking these statements over my life daily, a practice I continue to this day.

When I first started saying these statements, I did not believe them. In fact, I would almost cringe as I spoke them. After months of just saying them, however, I started believing them. They were who God said I was, after all; who was I to not believe God?

Despite this, on one occasion, I was struggling with my emotions and started feeling suicidal. In that moment I started telling myself all the negative "I am" statements I had previously spoken about myself.

Fortunately, God gave me the good sense to reach out to a friend. I had them read my Godly affirmations over me to help me get the bad thoughts out of my mind. The Bible says we are to "take every thought captive to the obedience of Christ." (2 Corinthians 10:5, NIV) The best way to do that is to know who you are in Christ. My friend created a wonderful pamphlet that shows a lot of the bible verses that say who we are in Christ. You can find this list at the end of this book or at www.jesusdidit.org.

At first saying positive words over yourself seems awkward but, after a time, you start to believe them. In fact, I started to fall in love with who I was, someone who was not only beautiful on the inside but the outside, as well. I stopped viewing myself in the negative way that others had told me I was and started living as the person God created me to be.

The day after I got my divorce from my second husband, I traded in my F150 and got my dream car, a yellow VW Bug convertible. I drove an hour from the dealership to my house with the convertible top down in the freezing cold. I could not stop smiling because, in this moment, I finally knew who I was. I had stopped trying to just make the world happy and started living for God. In that moment, even after divorce and heartbreak, my heart was full because I knew I was loved, worthy, strong, enough, beautiful, intelligent, highly favored, brave, creative, and created for a purpose.

"She threw away all her masks, and put on her soul."

-- Author Unknown

Day 18 Activity: Discovering Who You Really Are

Who are you? Who do you want to be? Compare with who God says you are.*

I am _____

I am _____

I am _____

I am _____

I am _____

I am _____

I am _____

I am _____

I am _____

I am _____

I am _____

I am _____

* Bible-based "I am" statements are listed at the end of this book.

HONESTY: THE BEST POLICY

Step 19: Acknowledging Past Failure

"Blows that hurt cleanse away evil, as do stripes the inner depths of the heart."

Proverbs 20:30

Any time a new fad diet came out, I was the first to start the diet. I would follow the diet strictly for a few weeks but, every time, each diet ended the same way: failure. That's because each time I would become frustrated with the lack of results, despite my strict observance of the rules, so I would cave into temptation and eat what I wanted. Sometimes I would fall into a pattern of starving myself for a few days, then binge eating on whatever I could get my hands on, usually pizza and ice cream. After each failed attempt, I felt worse about myself than when I started because this time, it was I, not the diet, that was a failure.

The first fad diet I tried was diet shakes. I was diligent about only having a shake for breakfast, a shake for lunch, and a healthy dinner. Soon, I found that my energy was low because I was not getting enough calories, yet I was hungry all the time. After a month of being on the diet, my cholesterol was tested. It was extremely high. My doctor said this was due to the shakes and advised me to stop using them. After a month of starving and being irritated, I had only lost five pounds.

Shortly thereafter I decided to try another diet program. Under this plan, an entire months' worth of food was delivered to your house in a box. The food was expensive and I was shocked at the portion sizes. They were extremely small and left me feeling hungry. I was determined to lose weight with this system, however, so I stuck to the plan, not altering it in any way. I became obsessed and started weighing myself both in the morning and at night. After just two months, I had lost 25 pounds. This wasn't good enough to satisfy me, however. I thought I wasn't shedding the excess weight fast enough, so I started skipping meals again, thinking that would help. Eventually, though I had to quit. The diet was too costly and I could no longer handle the constant feeling of being starved.

There were other fad diets I entertained, but most would last a week or two, then I would cave into temptation. I just could not resist food and the feeling of joy I had when I ate. Once I fell to temptation, I gave up, telling myself, "I'll try again tomorrow." This happened often enough, I even coined a phrase for the syndrome. I called it my "Tomorrow Diet." Of course, every time I quit a program, all the weight I'd lost came back on and often I'd put even more pounds on my tiny frame.

Being overweight also made it difficult for me to conceive. My first husband and I were determined to have a baby, however, so I tried once more to lose the excess poundage. When all my efforts failed, the doctor suggested gastric-bypass surgery.

In desperation I met with a surgeon and developed a plan for the surgery. A month before the surgery, they had me list all the foods I was eating. When I met again with the surgeon, he was shocked by how little I was eating. He advised I go see a counselor. The counselor helped me realize that I identified too much with being the "big girl." The surgery would, as a result, not help my mindset or fix my eating disorders. After months of consideration, I determined not to go further with the surgery. This turned out to be a blessing in disguise because it allowed me to realize, further down the road, that I could do it without surgery. I just had to change my mindset.

Shortly after walking away from the gastric bypass surgery, I joined Weight Watchers for the first time. I was doing really well on the program until I learned my first marriage was breaking apart. The emotional toll of trying to hold my marriage together led me into a deep depression. The only mode I used to cope was food. Soon everything I had lost with using the Weight Watchers method was gained back and, again, I added a lot more.

After my marriage ended I cared even less about my body and ate as much as I could. Food was my only source for comfort. Eventually I met my second husband. He loved big women and thus enabled me to continue my poor eating habits as this fulfilled his carnal desires.

I was failing because I was trying to change my body for all the wrong reasons: to look better, to have a baby, to fulfill the desires of my husband. I was not trying to lose it for myself. I wouldn't lose weight until I wanted to do it so I would feel better physically and mentally. I wouldn't lose weight until I believed that doing so would help me accomplish what God wanted me to do. Success would not be mine while the motivation was to feed the needs or desires of others.

On a positive note, I also learned that failure was not the opposite of success; it was part of it. All my failures God eventually used to help me understand myself more and become necessary stepping stones to success.

"Success is not final, failure is not fatal: it is the courage to continue that counts."

Winston Churchill

140

Step 19 Activity: Acknowledging Past Failure

What was your biggest failure in life?

_____

_____

_____

_____

What emotions do you have around failure?

_____

_____

_____

_____

What did you learn from past failures?

_____

_____

_____

_____

Step 20: Taking Ownership

Ezekiel 37:4 "Again He said to me, "Prophesy to these bones, and say to them, 'O dry bones, hear the word of the Lord!"

Ezekiel 37:4

For almost two years after my second marriage fell apart, I did not realize I was subconsciously trying to kill myself. Seven months after he left, I became a Christian but my habits with food and exercise did not change. I was reading the Bible and going to church but I was not honoring my body. Although I had become saved, I still was not delivered from my pain and hurt. I was a work in progress and God was walking me through a deliverance process that first started in my mind, then led to my physical transformation. First, however, I had to take ownership of my own life and stop blaming the world.

I had an underactive thyroid and polycystic ovarian syndrome which made my body process sugar worse than most. These conditions also caused me to be prone to being overweight and lethargic. Having failed so often in dieting, I finally decided to give up. If it was going to be twice as difficult for me to lose weight due to my body conditions, why even bother? So, after my second husband left me, I gave up completely.

My normal routine became coming home from work, ordering a pizza, eating half of it and saving the other half for the next night, and watching a program on Netflix. I had no social life and I wanted to die. I hid myself from the world as much as I could and I did not care about my weight. For lunch and breakfast I would order fast food. I did not want to cook for myself because I did not love myself enough to care for myself.

The day I decided to change came when I had trouble standing in the shower. I had so much trouble, in fact, that I ended up sitting on the edge of the tub to wash myself. My entire body, mind and spirit were was in pain, and I decided, then and there, did not want to live like this anymore. I cried in the restroom, feeling like a huge failure. Just then, I realized that no one else was around. No one else caused me to neglect myself. I had done this completely by myself.

Yes, there were outside factors that caused my emotional eating. Yes, my body had different struggles than most. No outside factor could give me the desire to make the change, however. The weight I was carrying was a direct reflection of all the pain that I had experienced in my life. If I truly wanted to heal, I had to find new ways to deal with my internal pain. I had to learn to trust God and myself. As I cried myself to sleep that night, I released all of my anxiety and fear over to God and asked Him to help me become accountable for my journey.

144

Throughout my life I had surrounded myself with people that needed me to care for them so I did not have to look at my own problems. As a former codependent I had learned that, by focusing my energy on needy people, I did not have to worry about solving my own emotional scars. Now the only person I had to care for was myself. No longer could I deflect my pain or ignore it. I had to face my problems head on.

In order to take ownership, I had to go back and look at my past failures. I had to realize that these failures were mine and I was the only one that could take control of my life through Jesus. I had to surrender to Jesus and allow Him to show me how to eat properly and deal with my emotions. There were nights when I wanted to give up and order pizza, but then I would remember that this would not help me get to where God wanted me to be. That was enough to stop me.

After a while, I recognized that acknowledging my brokenness gave me strength. When I was hiding from my problems and bottling them up, I would eat more and become lazy. As I started acknowledging that everything was not okay, I could finally heal not only my mind but my body. The realization that I had to take ownership of how I let the outside circumstances impact me was the pivotal point that allowed me to heal and brought real peace into my life. I could not change what had happened to me but I could change how I responded.

"But he said to me, "My grace is sufficient for you, for my power is made perfect in weakness." Therefore I will boast all the more gladly about my weaknesses, so that Christ's power may rest on me."

2nd Corinthians 12:9

Step 20 Activity: Taking Ownership

What areas of your life have you neglected?

1. _____
2. _____
3. _____
4. _____
5. _____

What impact has neglecting these areas of your life had on you?

_____

_____

_____

Forgive yourself for neglecting yourself.

BEGINNING YOUR HEALTHY RELATIONSHIP WITH FOOD

Step 21: Identifying Comfort Foods

"No temptation has overtaken you
except such as is common to man;
but God is faithful,
who will not allow you to be tempted
beyond what you are able,
but with the temptation will also make the way
of escape, that you may be able to bear it."

1 Corinthians 10:13

My dad was my entire world when I was little and I was, hands down, a daddy's girl. He was always there for me and encouraged every activity I participated in. When I was a cheerleader, he would learn the cheers and practice with me. If I had a school concert or event, he was always there. Any time I spent with my dad, I felt comfortable because he was safe. He never hit me or made fun of me. Instead, he encouraged me and loved me. I did not realize until years after he passed that he was abusive, as well, because he helped create an unhealthy living environment.

Food was a big deal in my house, especially for my dad. Because we were poor food was limited, so when we could afford to eat, we made sure it was food we liked. One time my sister and I were really hungry.

Unfortunately, the only food in the house was flour and unsweetened cocoa. That didn't stop us! We created our own version of chocolate pancakes from just those two ingredients. They were disgusting but we ate them anyway.

We often got creative with our food and food choices because resources were limited. Every summer we were left alone a lot, starting from a very young age. Our parents would give us each a dollar every day to buy our breakfast and dinner. My sister and I would go to the only store within walking distance, a little convenience store like the ones you'd find inside gas stations that don't have gas pumps. I would buy a bag of chips and my sister would buy a Little Debbie® snack. There were no other options for us in the store. We would split the food and still be hungry.

When we got the opportunity to eat good food and fill up, we did. Every Friday was a day we could fill up at dinner. Our mom worked night shift so our dad got to spend time alone with just us girls.

I looked forward to Friday night, not because of the upcoming weekend but because my dad would make sure we had a great evening. There was never any fighting or arguing on Fridays and, most importantly, we never went hungry. My dad would drive us into town, the oldies music turned up, singing and joking as we went to pick up our favorite pizza. Before the pizza was ready, we would head over to Dairy Queen® and pick up chocolate-dipped ice cream cones for dessert. We would spend the rest of the night watching movies and laughing.

It should come as no surprise that I came to equate pizza and ice cream with happiness. Later in life, whenever I felt stressed out, I would often run to those foods.

Early on in my relationship with my second husband we were in a heated argument that led to me crying. He knew my weakness so, in an attempt to comfort me, he offered to get me ice cream. I immediately calmed down. At that moment I was not even hungry but the moment the ice cream went into my mouth, I stopped crying and forgot about my hurt.

One of the happiest moments I had with my mom was when she taught me how to cook sausage biscuits and gravy. I cherish the happy moments with her because they were so few. On rare occasions that she would cook, the food was superb. She was addicted to food and her temper would subside when she was either cooking or eating food. In those moments I saw her laugh and be happy. I felt she loved me when she cooked for us. It was one of only a few ways she showed her love. Not surprisingly, I did the same thing when I was in a relationship. I overfed my partner in an attempt to show my love.

As I was healing from all the pain, I had to learn that food was not my comfort; God was. It took awhile but eventually, I realized that food did not make me feel better; it was a drug to numb the pain. I started to face rather than feed the pain and began figuring out which foods I used to comfort me and why. For example, pizza made me feel loved because that was the dinner my dad had gotten us on Friday nights. Sausage biscuits and gravy made me feel accepted because one of the rare times Mom showed me that she loved me was when she taught me that recipe. Ice cream brought me happiness because it also reminded me of joyful times on Friday nights. Each food I ate triggered some happy emotion in my brain, so when I was lacking that feeling, I would eat the food that represented the happy feeling I needed.

"Food is fuel, not therapy."

-- Author Unknown

Step 21 Activity: Identifying Comfort Foods

What foods do you love and why?

FOOD	Emotion Tied to It

Step 22: Breaking Up with Food

"Fear not, for I am with you;
Be not dismayed, for I am your God.
I will strengthen you,
Yes, I will help you,
I will uphold you with My righteous right hand."

Isaiah 41:10

I realized I had an issue with food when I sat in a grocery parking lot in the midst of a panic attack. I did not want to go into the store. I could not face all the temptation and stares of people as they secretly judged what was in my cart.

Everything about shopping in a grocery store overwhelmed me so I stopped shopping. Not only did I find it emotionally difficult; I struggled to walk every aisle. I knew I was not making the right decisions with my diet but I could not resist the temptation. I resorted to only ordering groceries online that would be delivered to my house or eating fast food.

I had so much shame about my eating habits that I did whatever I could to hide them from the world. I would never eat in public and avoided social situations that required everyone to look at me while I was eating. Eating was a secret, intimate event for me. It was a time where I could be alone and forget the world. There was

155

no judgment or pain when I ate, just pure bliss. Every time after I ate, however, I would feel guilty and ashamed. This pattern of medicating my emotions with food continued for years until, eventually, I was so good at hiding any of the times I ate, I even believed this was normal.

My wake up call came when I saw how much money I was spending on fast food each week. (I was spending around $200 a week on food. Now that I have gotten my eating under control I spend about $70 a week at the grocery store.) Although I loved to cook for others, I hated cooking for myself. I did not see the point of it. Yet whenever I fell into a deep depression, the only comfort I had was eating junk food.

At the lowest point of my life, when I was going through my second divorce, I was eating out for every meal. I did not want to face the reality that I was going through a second divorce, I was in my 30's and not where I wanted to be in life. I felt as if my life had no hope, so I did not want to care for myself. I used food as my therapist. I found joy when I felt full (after years of malnourishment, the connection is obvious). Only then could I finally go to sleep.

Unfortunately, my addiction to this unhealthy way of eating was also killing me. I knew that but I did not care. I wanted to die. This changed when I began knowing God more and understanding that I was worthy of love and acceptance. Before then, all I had ever felt was self-loathing and rejection.

Once I met the Lord, I felt accepted by God, and I knew I needed to break up with food. Not only did I need to do it; I actually wanted to do so. I also knew I needed help. So I prayed and asked God to direct me.

As I prayed God gave me a start date of March 5, 2017. This gave me two weeks to prepare for my breakup with emotional eating. My journey would start on a Sunday before church at a Weight Watchers meeting. In preparation I cleaned out my fridge and cabinets. I took all the food I knew was unhealthy and gave it away.

I started with clean new habits, setting ground rules that would help me stay the course this time. Since pizza was my favorite vice, I did not allow myself to have pizza delivered anymore. To this day I still have not had a pizza delivered to me. Another vice of mine was fast food, so I decided not to allow myself to get it unless it was a salad without dressing. Due to the cost of the salads at fast food restaurants, I quickly learned even salads were not worth buying there.

Although it may seem silly, I wrote food a break up letter. This letter helped me get out the reasons why I loved food, why I was stronger now, and why I did not need to rely on food. Today, whenever I feel tempted by unhealthy food, I look at the pros and cons. I decided if the enjoyment of the food is worth the end result.

On occasion I will treat myself to one of these favorite forbidden foods. I did not eat pizza for four months prior to my New York City trip, for example. When I was in New York, however, I allowed myself to have one slice. Over time, I have learned that food does not heal my problems; it just creates more of them, especially if I overuse food.

I also learned how to comfort myself in other ways than eating. Today, walking and painting are two of my favorite ways to alleviate stressful emotions. I've also started making friends and getting closer to God. When my trials get extremely overwhelming, I put on worship music and dance. Before, I used food to battle my depression. Now I have found much healthier ways to deal with the same.

"You don't cure emotional eating by removing all comfort foods. You do it by learning to comfort yourself"

-- Author Unknown

Day 22 Activity: Breaking Up with Food

1. Clean out your fridge/pantry
2. Shop the outside isles
3. Find ways to cope
4. Find other ways to celebrate
5. Do not look for recipes online
6. Write a break-up note to food. Here's a template you can use:

Dear Comfort Food:

Thank you for providing me with feelings of _____. My foods of choice were

_____
_____. I no longer need these foods to feel _____. I will use food as a form of fuel with the occasional treat. I will not use my comfort food for pain or joy and I break the codependency with unhealthy food. I will use _____ to cope instead.

Step 23: Tracking Your Diet

"Therefore, having these promises, beloved, let us cleanse ourselves from all filthiness of the flesh and spirit, perfecting holiness in the fear of God."

2 Corinthians 7:1

For many years, I thoroughly believed I was not an overeater. No one could tell me I was overeating because I was ordering "meals" at fast food restaurants and I was not eating all of the pizza, just half. Compared to my friends I was eating just as much as them or less. I had no idea I was an overeater until I started tracking my food (writing down what I ate at each meal in a little notebook). Not only was I an overeater; I was an overeater of the wrong foods.

I could not believe I was 35 years old and I had no idea how to eat properly or how much I needed to eat. My favorite breakfast was a Starbucks® java chip Frappuccino with a bagel and cream cheese. This was not a lot of food but the calorie content was astronomical. After starting Weight Watchers® I had to slowly make changes to the way I was eating and find alternatives to my food. I also learned to love fruits and vegetables.

Tracking my food made me really see what I was eating wrong and where I needed to make changes. Through months of tracking my food, I learned what worked for my body and what did not. Every individual's body is different but by tracking your weight and your food help you determine what changes you will have to make.

As I mentioned before I love bagels so, during my journey, I found a Weight-Watchers® friendly bagel option that used a fourth a cup of self-rising flour and a fourth a cup of nonfat unflavored Greek yogurt. The bagel was only three points so I felt freedom to eat it. Unfortunately, that week I gained weight even though I was in my caloric goal. My body processes flour different than other bodies and I learned to eat flour on rare occasions.

Tracking your food is not a punishment or a control issue, by the way. It's just a helpful tool in helping you see how your body responds to food. Today my diet consists mainly of vegetables and lean meat because that is what makes me feel the most satisfied and helps me lose the most weight.

At first tracking seemed like a big hassle but now I find it fun discovering ways to modify my diet to make eating exciting and different. I love to cook for myself now because I know I can get better quality food at lower cost and with more nutritional value.

I also realized as I started tracking my food that I actually ate more throughout the day but still lost weight because I was eating food that fueled my body, not my

162

emotions. By eating throughout the day, I was also changing my metabolism. Here is an example of a typical day of eating for me:

Breakfast - Two eggs, fruit, and coffee

Snack 1 – One egg and a vegetable (usually cucumber)

Lunch - Salad with lean meat (usually boneless skinless chicken breast) and Olive Garden® low-fat Italian dressing.

Snack 2 - A piece of fruit

DInner - Boneless skinless chicken breast with a lot of vegetables

Dessert – Sugar-free popsicle

Some of my favorite snacks are apples with cinnamon, English muffin with spray butter and light jam, air-popped popcorn, pretzels, Halo Top® ice cream and Popchips®.

Do not get discouraged when you first start to track your food intake and weight. Look at it as a way to collect information, not a list meant to criticize you. For example, I had to learn to look at the number on the bathroom scale as a reference point, not an identification of who I was. Tracking empowers us to make changes so we can feel better about ourselves, not a tool meant to condemn us.

"It is not a diet: it is a long term lifestyle change."

-- Author Unknown

Day 23 Activity: Tracking Your Diet

Find a program that works for you and start tracking your food.

	Sun	Mon	Tues	Wed	Thurs	Fri	Sat
Bkfast							
Snack							
Lunch							
Snack							
Dinner							
Snack							

Note: There are a lot of free tracking devices online. I personally use Weight Watchers®. Myfitnesspal® has also received a lot of good reviews.

YOU'VE GOT TO MOVE IT, MOVE IT!

Step 24: Get Moving

"The soul of a lazy man desires, and has nothing; But the soul of the diligent shall be made rich."

Proverbs 13:4

My inability to stand and walk was causing me to stay away from activities I loved such as hiking, going to festivals with friends, walking on the beach, and much more. I could not stand for more than five minutes and the physical pain in my body was impacting my job performance. At one point I had pain in my back that was so severe that, when I would walk to greet a member at the bank or run to get an item for someone, I would almost be in tears. I tried to mask the pain but I am sure it was reflected in the grimace on my face. I knew I had to make a change and it was going to be painful.

You have to move your body. I started by walking short distances; each step was painful. I began by walking along the Puget Sound at a spot called Owen's Beach because I knew there was a bench every 1000 feet.

The first time I walked this 1.5 mile stretch I thought I was going to die. I sat down at every bench I came across for a few moments. I felt bad about how out of shape I was; it made me even more determined to change. I set a goal of getting out and moving more. Now I can walk that trail without stopping once and see it as more of a warm up then a work out. It is not uncommon for me to walk four miles in one session.

You will feel sore and have some pain when you start to move and work out but realize that this pain will not last forever and the results are worth the pain. I was embarrassed about going to the gym. Working out in front of others made me feel inadequate. Nevertheless, I joined Planet Fitness® a month into my weight loss journey I remember my first experience of getting on an elliptical machine. A much more fit person got onto the elliptical next to me and was using it at Level 10, where resistance is strenuous and the incline is steep. They did so, breathing easily. In comparison, I was using the machine at Level 2 and panting profusely. My face must have been covered in defeat because she looked at me and said, "In a year you will not be struggling as much as you are today. Just keep going. Remember you are doing more now than you would be sitting on the couch." Although these words are not that poetic and would not be plastered on a motivational poster ,they have stuck with me. Some movement -- any movement -- is better than doing nothing.

As I started moving more, I noticed that my mental health was improving as well. Today, as I work out, usually pray and listen to Christian music. I feel twenty times better after I work out and I actually crave physical exercise where, before, I loathed and dreaded it. I try different things to switch up my routine and often I ask friends to join me. Walking remains my favorite activity because it costs nothing and most people can do it. I have found a lot of fun trails to walk in the Pacific Northwest section of the United States where I live. One of my favorites is the Tacoma Narrows Bridge. The first time I decided to walk that bridge I could only walk half of it and had to stop many times. Now I can walk the entire bridge without stopping.

The Mayo Clinic sums up the 7 benefits of exercising on regular basis as follows:

1. Exercise controls weight
2. Exercise combats health conditions and diseases
3. Exercise improves mood
4. Exercise boosts energy
5. Exercise promotes better sleep
6. Exercise puts the spark back in your sex life
7. Exercise can be fun and social.

You can read more at https://www.mayoclinic.org/healthy-lifestyle/fitness/in-depth/exercise/art-20048389.

It is going to be difficult when you first start moving. Find activities you like to do. Ask someone else to do the activities with you if you like. When you start to get bored with an activity, do something different. Just start moving your body and your mind will feel better.

"To enjoy the glow of good health, you must exercise."

-- Gene Tunney, World Heavyweight Boxing Champion, 1926-1928

Step 24 Activity: Get Moving

What activities do you like to do?

_____

_____

_____

10 Ways to Move More:

1. Park further away from your destination.
2. Walk the store aisles once before you shop.
3. Walk during your lunch break.
4. Use the stairs.
5. Do wall sits while brushing your teeth.
6. Do calf raises while waiting in line.
7. Jog in place while waiting for the microwave or during commercials.
8. Walk while on the phone.
9. Set a timer to remember to move.
10. Instead of meeting a friend for coffee, meet for a walk.

What tasks can you add to your day to move more?

_____

_____

_____

Step 25: Commit to Move

"But let him ask in faith, with no doubting, for he who doubts is like a wave of the sea driven and tossed by the wind."

James 1:6

I have always had the mentality that, if someone else can do it, why can't I? This explains why I was a cheerleader even though I was the biggest girl on the squad. I danced even when I knew people were looking at me funny because of my size. I also did not care what people thought of me in my bathing suit. I knew people would judge me either way so I just owned my large body and did what I wanted to do. Due to my personality I draw attention wherever I go. I decided to use this for my benefit when I decided to commit to move.

One day I saw a video about a girl who exercised 100 days straight. Like me she was overweight and was not use to exercising. I decided I would exercise 100 days straight starting on June 1, 2017. At the time I did not realize my 100th day would be in New York City while I was visiting a few of my online friends for the first time. Each day for 100 days I worked out for at least 45 minutes. Luckily most of the 100 days were in the summer and I was able to walk outside.

I have always loved to take pictures so I decided to document my journey of exercising 100 days straight by taking pictures of the scenery. Every day I would upload pictures to my Twitter® feed showing the sites I saw. Sharing helped inspired others to get out and move more and helped me stay on track because I knew others were watching.

Completing 100 days of exercise had its challenges, especially on days when I had to work overtime due to meetings. Many times that meant I was out until 11:00 P.M. at night exercising. I was determined to not let anything stop me from hitting my goal, however, so no matter how late I finished work, I still exercised afterwards.

The worst day I experienced was one in which I had a staff meeting at 7 A.M. That meant I had to get up at 5:30 AM so I could exercise before work. The day also included two after-work meetings, meaning I would not be free until 10 P.M. that night. Still I went walking. Since it was late at night, I went to a local walking path that is lit and full of shops. I was exhausted when I finished, but I was ecstatic, too. I had finished. The results of fulfilling that exercise, no matter what? I lost 52 pounds in 100 days and I went down three dress sizes.

Another way I committed to exercise more was by buying a step-tracking device. My choice was a Fitbit®. I linked my Fitbit® with my friends' Fitbits® so I could compete with them to see who could walk the most steps. The first day I got my Fitbit® I barely walked 5,000 steps. I could not imagine ever completing 10,000 steps in one day. Slowly but surely, however, my average number of steps continued to increase. I was excited when I finally averaged 7,000 steps. I did not know at the time that today my average would be 14,000 steps. In fact, when I only walk 10,000 steps on a particular day, I feel like I have had a slow day. Imagine that!

Commitment is the key to being successful in this endeavor. Make a plan to exercise and set a goal. Exercising is a lot like tracking food. Every individual's body is different. Track your exercise in the same way you would your food. See what works well for you.

I would also suggest getting a personal trainer if you can afford one. If you can't afford one, work with a doctor or nutritionist. They can help you determine how much you should exercise. Walking is safe for most people. Listen to your body and take your time. Every step you take is better than not being active. You will build up your strength as long as you stay committed to the process.

"Most people fail not because of their lack of desire but because of their lack of commitment."

-- Coach Vince Lombardi

Day 25 Activity: Commit to Move

When can you spare some time to exercise?

_____

_____

_____

Set a schedule of activities you plan to do, when you plan to do them, and for how long.

Activity	MON	TUES	WED	THURS	FRI

Step 26: Challenge Yourself

"The lazy man will not plow because of winter;
He will beg during harvest and have nothing."

Proverbs 20:4

Try something you have never done before. Just because you have never been able to do it before doesn't mean you can't accomplish the challenge now. As I stated before, walking to the mailbox, only 200 feet from my house, was a huge task for me when I started my weight loss journey. I met with my friend before I started. She challenged me to set up goals along the way. At the time I thought it would be impossible for me to walk a 5K race. Then, in April 2017, I found Bubble Run, a 5K walk that would be held about three months from then. I did not know how I was going to get off the couch to compete in a 5K walk but I decided to sign up anyway.

I shared my vision with a few close friends and began to train. Using my Fitbit® I kept track of my walking, slowly increasing my steps daily. I checked in with friends on my progress and continued to challenge myself. On July 22, 2017, I went to the Puyallup Fairgrounds and walked the 5K in advance of the race. This would be the first time I would be walking a 5K race, after all.

Being an obese woman I hated crowds because I felt people were staring at me. I was determined to finish the race, however, so off I went for a test run. I squeezed into my shirt and put on some music to help me get through the course. Yes, I felt embarrassed as people passed by but I was determined to remain focused and on task.

Finally, the actual day of the Bubble Run arrived. I had a lot as anxiety when I started because I did not know if I could finish. There wasn't anybody with me to cheer me on, either.

The course was decorated with what organizers called "Bubble Stations" all along the way. I used them to help me stay motivated, as it helped break up the distance and I could tell myself, "Okay, now get to the next set of colored bubbles." A friend also kept checking in on me via phone as I went.

As I crossed the finish line, I was so proud of myself. I went to the after party where they had a ton of bubbles to play in. For the first time in a long time, I was able to dance and smile because I had worked for something and was able to accomplish what I thought at the beginning would be impossible.

The trick to staying productive on my weight loss journey, I have found, is finding different ways to challenge myself. Another challenge I did was The Big Climb. The Big Climb is a stair climb up the Columbia

Center, the tallest skyscraper in downtown Seattle. There are 69 floors of stairs, 1311 steps, and 788 feet of vertical elevation. This was a challenge for me to say the least because I could barely walk 7 stairs without getting out of breath when I started my journey.

I trained for four months for The Big Climb (the event supports leukemia research), setting a plan that would help me increase my stair count daily. I started by using the stair climbing machine at the gym.

At first I could only go up 30 flights of stairs, but every few days I increased that number until I could complete 70 flights of stairs. When I first got to 70 flights of stairs, it took me 34 minutes. When I finished training for the The Climb, I was getting 70 fights done in just under 20 minutes.

There were a lot of tears, sweat, and pain as I trained but the challenge changed me physically and mentally. Despite all that training, I was not prepared for the dizziness of going around and around from staircase to staircase that ensued when I actually competed on March 25, 2018 in The Climb. I also wasn't prepared for the elevation gain. When I reached flight 64, I thought I was going to pass out. I sat for a moment and decided to continue the climb. When I finished I was dizzy and my lips were blue but I finished in 31 minutes.

In order to be successful, we have to set SMART goals. The Big Climb in the Columbia Center was a SMART goal because it was:

S - Specific - I chose to enter The Big Climb, an actual event in real time.

M- Measurable - I needed to climb to the top of 69 flights of stairs.

A - Attainable – It showed me physically able to climb 69 flights of stairs.

R - Relevant - The Big Climb would help me in my weight loss journey.

T - Time bound - The Big Climb would happen on March 25, 2018.

We have to make sure we are making SMART goals for our challenges. Only when they are practical, measurable, relevant to our journey, and challenging to us personally will they benefit us the most as we seek to make ultimate beneficial changes in our lives.

"If it does not challenge you it does not grow you."

-- Author Unknown

Step 26 Activity: Challenge Yourself

Complete a challenge for yourself. Use the Smart Method to choose and plan what you will do.

Specific _____

Measurable _____

Attainable _____

Relevant _____

Time Bound _____

184

EXECUTING YOUR PLAN

Day 27: Allowing God to Work

*"As iron sharpens iron,
So a man sharpens the countenance of his friend."*

Proverbs 27:17

Sometimes when we start a journey we have no idea on how we are going to accomplish a seemingly overwhelming goal. I had no idea how I was going to lose over 200 pounds but I now see God was directing my path and setting me up for the miracles placed in my life.

We have to allow God to work. When you submit your needs to God in prayer, He will direct your journey and show you how He can help you make the impossible possible.

When my husband left me, I had no support system at all. When I gave God control of my journey, however, He placed people in my life to encourage me all along the way.

The week of June 1, 2017, I saw God's support for me evidenced in a particularly memorable way. As you may recall, this was during the same season that I decided to commit to 100 days of exercise.

In May I went work as I normally did. A woman came into the bank who had some questions about her account. I noticed she looked extremely fit and was wearing pearl earrings. I, too, happened to be wearing pearl earrings that day, a gift that a friend had just sent me in the mail.

After I told her that I loved her earrings, we started talking about pearls and what they meant. That's when she mentioned God. I rarely talk about God at work but I was feeling led to talk to her more. Just then, I heard the Holy Spirit tell me to ask her if she were a personal trainer. Though I felt awkward in asking, I obeyed. Amazingly, she was.

We parted ways and I thought nothing further of the conversation. Then, during that first week of June, I received an email from her stating that God had led her to give me 12 free sessions. That's three whole months of training for free! I was amazed and humbly accepted.

This was not all God did for me during this short time period. That same week as I was weighing in at Weight Watchers®, the instructor said, "Congratulations! Because you lost 10 pounds in your first three months here, you can receive either $100 or 3 months of free Weight Watchers®. I chose the three months of free Weight Watchers® because it was equal to $132.

As if that were not enough, I went into my local gym and I saw the lady who signed me up. It had been a few months since I'd seen her so she could see my 40-pound weight loss. I told her about how I managed to lose the weight, then went to go exercise.

As I was on the elliptical, she walked over and told me the gym was proud of my journey and had decided to award me with -- you guessed it – three months of free membership at the gym. All of this happened during the three months leading up to my New York City trip, another event I'd scheduled to help me in my journey to wholeness and a whole new me.

Thinking back on this experience and the miracles God worked on my behalf reminds me that, if we allow God to work, He will do the impossible. We just have to make our request known to Him. We have to commit to Him. Then, for every bit of investment and hard work we put in, God will put in that much more. To this day I am in disbelief over the favor that the Lord has show me in my journey. My journey is not for myself alone, however; it is all for Him and His glory.

"God is fighting your battles, arranging things in your favor, making a way even when you don't see a way."

-- Joel Osteen

Step 27 Activity: Allowing God to Work

Get away for as long as or as little as you want and be silent and listen to God.

What is God saying to you?

_____

_____

_____

_____

_____

What do you need to hand over to God?

_____

_____

_____

Step 28: Allowing Grace

" But may the God of all grace, who called us to His eternal glory by Christ Jesus, after you have suffered a while, perfect, establish, strengthen, and settle you."

1 Peter 5:10

"What! I am up 3 pounds? How did that happen? I used the stair climber every day and I stayed within my points!" I had gained the most weight I ever had in one week. My Weight Watchers® instructor smiled, saying, :"It must be muscle," yet I was still frustrated.

The next week I was even more determined to exercise and eat right. Nevertheless, when my time to weigh in came, I had gained another two pounds! "You have got to be kidding me!" I said aloud. In two weeks I was up five pounds. I felt like a failure and that I disappointed God. As I sat down to wait for our weekly meeting to begin, I prayed, asking God to help me understand why I was gaining.

The past two weeks had been emotionally difficult. My divorce from my second husband was finalizing. Although I was ready for the change, I had fought for three years to save the marriage. Even though I felt ready, I was stressed out.

This time, however, I decided not to give into my cravings for pizza but continue doing what I knew was right. I focused my attention back on God and the journey rather than give into the despair at seeing my second marriage end. I decided to be kind to myself and allow grace to cover me.

There are many battles we must fight in order to win the war. If we give up every time we lose a battle, we will never reach our important goals in life. If I had given up in that moment, I would have not have won the war. The week after I decided to keep fighting despite my discouragement, I lost 6.6 pounds.

This taught me an important lesson: the scale won't always reflect the work you put in; it's just a tracking mechanism used to evaluate your progress. I had to look at the entire picture and, when the scale showed a gain, see what I do to change. In this weight loss journey, there will always be ups and downs, but we have to realize that the journey to health and wholeness, no matter what, is beautiful.

There were times I wanted to give up. At one point I was so distraught that I went to the grocery store and put every single food I wanted -- canned cheese, pizza, bagels, brownies, muffins, chips – into my cart. In my mind I said "Forget this journey! I'd rather be fat." Then, just as I was about to check out with my horde of unhealthy comfort food, I heard God say, "No! This is not how this chapter ends! Put those items back!" I put every single item back on the shelves and left the store. Then I called my accountability partner and we talked about why I felt like giving up. She was able to remind me of all the progress I had made. We said a prayer and I was back on track.

There will be times you want to give up, too; times you'll want to cave in. Know that such times are normal and you will get through those times of defeat.

Another frustration I had was with watching people eating food I wanted to eat. At first I would not allow myself to have anything off the plan. I quickly learned that, if this was going to be a lifestyle change, I would need to have grace in my diet. Now I do not skip the birthday cake; I just modify my portion. If there is pizza I will have a slice with a big salad instead of eating four slices. We are allowed to treat ourselves, just not overindulge in food.

Grace is not allowing bad behavior to happen when you hit a rough patch. It's being kind to yourself when you do have a bad weigh in, day, or meal. If we do not extend grace to ourselves in such times, we will give up whenever we think we've failed. Allow God to show you where you need to give yourself more grace on this journey and continue to ask Him to reveal to you what you need to change as you go along.

"Courage is grace under pressure."
-- Ernest Hemingway

193

Step 28 Activity: Allowing Grace

How are you still talking negatively about yourself?

1. _____

2. _____

3. _____

4. _____

5. _____

How will you allow grace in your journey?

_____

_____

_____

_____

Share these with your accountability partners so they can hold you accountable.

Step 29: Establishing Your Game Plan

"For which of you, intending to build a tower, does not sit down first and count the cost, whether he has enough to finish it—"
Luke 14:28

In March 2017 my friend decided to host a party where we created a vision board. A vision board contains our goals and aspirations in picture form on a board where we can see them at a glance.

As I was making my vision board, I found pictures of fruits and vegetables, weight loss, flowers, walking paths, adventure, and encouraging words. I made a collage of all the pictures and hung it in my front room so I would always have a visual reminder of my weight-loss goal.

We have to set goals in order to know where we want to be. When I saw the large number staring back at me that first day I weighed in at Weight Watchers®, I knew that was not where I wanted to stay. I sat with a weight loss counselor at Weight Watchers® and, based on my build and height, we determined my goal weight: 180 pounds.

Shortly after that I met with another counselor. She helped me work on my fears of losing weight and the emotional traumas related to losing it. I then put together my plan. In the Day 29 activity you will use the previous chapters to establish your game plan. Here was what my game plan looked like:

On March 5, 2017, my weight was XXXX pounds. My goal weight is 180 pounds. The reason I want to lose weight is to honor God and be able to move more freely. My accountability partners are my two best friends. I will talk daily with one of my best friends about my weight loss and meet weekly with my other best friend. I will also go to weekly Weight Watchers® meetings to check in and track my weight. I will place motivational quotes around my house and carry my charms (Weight Watchers® gives little items called "charms" out whenever you reach a milestone) with me. I will track my food using Weight Watchers®. I will exercise at least five days a week and aim to walk 10,000 steps each day. I will ask God daily to point out anything I need to modify.

Remember: your plan will vary and change as you go. As we travel on this journey, it is important to be flexible and add challenge to your plan. Allow God to change your thinking on how you are currently losing weight and getting healthy. This is not a smooth journey. It will have many hills and valleys. Having a set plan. However, will always enable us to evaluate our progress. This is not a pass or fail adventure. As long as you have not given up, you are successful.

"By failing to prepare you are preparing to fail."
-- Benjamin Franklin

Day 29 Activity: Establishing a Game Plan

1. My goal weight _____ (Day 2 activity)
2. This is important to me because of
   _____ (Day 3 activity)
3. My accountability partners are _____ and
   _____ (Day 4 activity)
4. I will post my "I am" statements _____
   and I will read them daily. (Day 18 activity)
5. I will track my food using _____ (Day
   23 activity)
6. I will exercise _____ per week. (Day 25
   activity)
7. I will get alone with God every _____ and listen.
   (Day 26 activity)

Step 30: Embracing the Journey

"For I know the thoughts that I think toward you, says the Lord, thoughts of peace and not of evil, to give you a future and a hope."

Jeremiah 29:11

As I was out shopping with a friend, I fell in love with a teal dress I found. I was sure it would not fit since it was a size 18. I had not been a size 18 since high school. My friend encouraged me to try the dress on anyway. To my disbelief it fit! I sat in the dressing room crying with happiness. I could not believe I was smaller than I had been in high school. My body had changed so much in this journey and would continue to do so. Just when I thought I could not possibly lose more, I did.

I struggled to recognize who I was becoming. On another occasion I was shopping with a friend who I always considered to be in a healthy weight range. I was stunned when I realized we were shopping in the same section. I was the same size as my healthy friend.

It still is difficult not to see myself as the fat girl. When I go into restaurants I still expect them to ask me "Table or booth?" Now they just give me a booth. When I go on an airplane, I still worry about the seat belt fitting without adding an extension, but it fits.

This journey continues to teach me that anything is possible and that, if we allow God to change our mindset, we can and will have a beautiful life. God has not only helped me lose weight; He has cured me from polycystic ovary syndrome, post-traumatic stress disorder, and major depression. He has brought me a support system and He has taught me to love. To embrace the journey is to allow God to transform us from the inside out.

Embrace the journey you are on and take pictures along the way. I used to be afraid of the camera but now I am a new creation in Christ. I want to be part of the picture. For years I was ashamed of who I was internally and externally but God has made me beautiful right where I am. I still have insecurities about my body but I do not allow my insecurities to define me. I share my experience with the world because God has done so much for me and this is a never-ending process.

There is no finish line in this journey, only a series of events that are beautiful if you allow yourself to see the beauty in them. God will be with you even in your darkest moments if you allow Him to me. This journey starts with a willingness to take one step each day toward a better future, both physically and mentally.

"Trust the wait. Embrace the uncertainty.
Enjoy the beauty of becoming.
When nothing is certain, anything is possible."
-- Author Unknown

Step 30 Activity: Embracing the Journey

Allow yourself to get excited about the journey.

Who will you share your journey with?

_____

_____

_____

_____

_____

Who Does the Bible Say You Are?

- A child of God (Romans 8: 14,15)
- A new creation in Christ (2 Corinthians 5:17)
- A saint (Ephesians 1:1)
- God's workmanship created in Christ for good works (Ephesians 2:10)
- A citizen of Heaven (Ephesians 2:19)
- A member of Christ's body (1 Corinthians 3:16)
- A friend of Christ (John 15:15)
- The righteousness of God in Christ (2 Corinthians 5:21)
- Righteous and holy (Ephesians 4:24)
- Chosen of God (Colossians 3:12-13)
- More than a conqueror through Christ (Romans 8:37)
- A chosen generation, a royal priesthood, a holy nation (1 Peter 2:9)
- Seated in heavenly places in Christ (Ephesians 2:4-6)
- A recipient of every spiritual blessing in the heavenly places (Ephesians 1-4)
- Redeemed by the blood of the Lamb (Revelations 5:9)
- Complete in Him who is the head of all principality and power (Colossians 2:10)
- Holy and without blame before Him in love (Ephesians 1:4, 1 Peter 1:16)
- Have the mind of Christ (1Corinthians 2:16; Philippians 2:5)
- Have the peace of God that passes all understanding (Philippians 4:7)
- An ambassador for Christ (2 Corinthians 5:20)
- Forgiven of all my sins and washed in the Blood (Ephesians 1:7)

- Delivered from the power of darkness and translated into God's Kingdom (Colossians 1:13)
- Healed by the stripes of Jesus (1 Peter 2:24)
- Bought with a price (1 Corinthians 6:20)
- Have access in one Spirit to the Father (Ephesians 2:18)
- The aroma of Christ to God among those who are being saved those perishing (2 Corinthians 2:15)
- Set free from sin, have become slaves of righteousness (Romans 6:18)
- Fearfully and wonderfully made (Psalm 139:14)
- Sealed for the day of redemption (Ephesians 4:30)

www.jesusdidit.org

Made in the USA
Middletown, DE
19 November 2018